"The love that Jesus has for His Church is immeasurable, and His commitment to her is unsurpassable. Written from the mind of a scholar and the heart of a pastor, this book will renew our love for Christ's Bride and lead to revelation of how He is reforming and beautifying His people in these last days. I cannot recommend this book highly enough!"

Lee M. Cummings, founder and senior leader, Radiant Church and Radiant Network; author, *School of the Spirit* and *Flourish: Planting Your Life Where God Designed It to Thrive*

"Are you a romantic at heart? Then this book is for *you*. My dear friend David Sliker shows how God's invitation to holiness and beauty fulfills our deepest desires. This book will give you a vision for being immersed in a love so expansive that every longing to be known is satisfied. Get ready for the beauty realm!"

Bob Sorge, author, *Secrets of the Secret Place*

The
TRIUMPH
of
BEAUTY

The
TRIUMPH
of
BEAUTY

GOD'S RADIANT
ANSWER
FOR THE WORLD'S
GROWING DARKNESS

DAVID SLIKER

Chosen
a division of Baker Publishing Group
Minneapolis, Minnesota

© 2022 by David Sliker

Published by Chosen Books
11400 Hampshire Avenue South
Minneapolis, Minnesota 55438
www.chosenbooks.com

Chosen Books is a division of
Baker Publishing Group, Grand Rapids, Michigan

Printed in the United States of America

Library of Congress Cataloging-in-Publication Data
Names: Sliker, David, author.
Title: The triumph of beauty : God's radiant answer for the world's growing darkness / David Sliker.
Description: Minneapolis, Minnesota : Chosen Books, a division of Baker Publishing Group, [2022] | Includes bibliographical references.
Identifiers: LCCN 2022014605 | ISBN 9780800761936 (trade paper) | ISBN 9780800762674 (casebound) | ISBN 9781493435838 (ebook)
Subjects: LCSH: Aesthetics—Religious aspects—Christianity. | Violence—Religious aspects—Christianity.
Classification: LCC BR115.A8 S625 2022 | DDC 261.5/7—dc23/eng/20220504
LC record available at https://lccn.loc.gov/2022014605

Cover design by Rob Williams, InsideOut Creative Arts, Inc.

Baker Publishing Group publications use paper produced from sustainable forestry practices and post-consumer waste whenever possible.

22 23 24 25 26 27 28   7 6 5 4 3 2 1

To the Intercessors of the
International House of Prayer,
my beloved spiritual family.

This is your story, and I am honored beyond measure
that I get to run with ones such as you,
of whom the world is not worthy.

Thank you for your ceaseless reach
for the fullness of God
and His promises for this generation.
You are heroes of the faith to me,
and I will cherish our time together, forever.

CONTENTS

FOREWORD

Have you ever wondered why shows like *Fixer Upper* and *Top Chef* are so incredibly popular? We seemingly never tire of watching a skilled craftsman take a dilapidated, mold-ridden shack and turn it into a mansion. Or watching a consummate artist with food take a bunch of ostensibly incompatible ingredients and turn them into a gorgeous feast for the senses.

The reason is that humans are deeply and innately fascinated by the process of turning chaos into order, brokenness into beauty, a mess into a masterpiece.

This creative process captivates and satisfies us because this is, in fact, what we are created for. Genesis describes the original design and purpose for humanity as *cultivation*—taking the raw, messy, chaotic elements of the world and, in partnership with the Creator, shaping them into order, beauty and flourishing.

Yet in falling into sin, we ceased to be mess fixers and became mess makers. Instead of being partners with God, we became His prodigals, squandering our inheritance, purpose and destiny.

In response, Jesus our Elder Brother journeyed to the wasteland we had made of the world, ransomed us from our spiritual bondage, reconciled us to the Father and, like a patient and methodical master craftsman, began the greatest restoration project in history. First, He is restoring us, His Church, and then through us, as we partner with Him, He will restore the world.

For so many Christians, however, this sounds like a frankly unbelievable story. When we look at ourselves and the world around us, we struggle to perceive how this great Artist is supposedly working in so much mess to create something beautiful.

The real problem is that *we don't know Him*. When we're watching a TV show, we feel confident that the craftsman or chef in charge knows what he or she is doing, and the messier things get, the more excited we become anticipating the miraculous transformation the expert will pull off. When it comes to Jesus' creative restoration in our lives and in the world, however, we don't feel that same confidence.

But we can have that confidence. This is the primary purpose of Scripture—to show us the nature of this great Artist who is at work in us and in the world, making all things new and beautiful in His time. The psalmist tells us that God has a plan for our lives and for human history, and that this plan is the only plan that will ultimately be accomplished and last for eternity: "The LORD brings the counsel of the nations to nothing; He makes the plans of the peoples of no effect. The counsel of the LORD stands forever, the plans of His heart to all generations" (Psalm 33:10–11).

The Triumph of Beauty is an incredible gift to believers in this generation. It takes the revelation of who God is and His unshakable plan in our lives, revealed in Scripture, and provides the *clarity* and *context* we need to actually see God at work in us and through us—right here and right now.

There is perhaps no greater need in the Body of Christ right now than for us to receive this revelation. When we see God with clarity and context, it cuts through the chaos and confusion of the human narratives that bombard us, it awakens our hearts to the love and purpose for which we were created, and it fills us with courage and faith to trust God and partner with Him in this great masterpiece of restoration. What He is up to is better than any show, story or adventure we could ever come up with, and He doesn't just want us to watch it—He wants us to live it and create it with Him. There is nothing more fascinating, captivating, awe-inspiring or beautiful than that.

Banning Liebscher

INTRODUCTION

All Things Beautiful

This is a book about beauty.

Specifically, the beauty of the Church around the world, in one generation, before the Lord returns. This is a book about the beauty of God being imparted to His people everywhere—to the ones who sincerely love Him and want to be pleasing to Him as they walk out loving Him and others. The full potential of the Church, realized in the grace of God, is a force to be reckoned with in opposition to the wicked powers of this world. The Church has a destiny that involves a glorious witness to the world regarding who Jesus really is and what He is really like.

Therefore, you have a great and glorious future filled with beauty, pleasure, joy and profound satisfaction in walking out the fullness of the Father's commands, experiencing His Son's love and engaging in the power of His Spirit. Any book about the Church is a book about you and the future that burns in the heart of the Father for you. Your story, as we will see, is our shared story. It is both weak, broken and small, and significant, eternal and powerful at the same exact time. In a critical moment in history, God has a glorious plan involving His beauty and His people, and that plan is designed to get the attention of the nations by advertising who He really is and what He is really like. In other words, the destiny I spoke of in the previous paragraph is not a far-off, future one. The time for the unfolding plans of God to purify, beautify and bring His Church into maturity in love is right here, right now. He wants you to be right in the middle of it.

God's plans are just in time. The world is growing significantly uglier, and it is happening very quickly.

Our awareness and personal connection to the ugliness is growing at an uncomfortably exponential rate. If you are older, you might agree that the explosion of lawlessness, corruption, oppression, looting and beyond feels different from the protests and unrest of the 1960s. It feels fundamentally different from the malaise of the late 1970s, the greed of the 1980s, the financial corruption and meltdown of the 1990s and the first decade of this current century. What seemed grassroots in the 1960s, or segmented in the decades that followed, now seems to be impacting everyone, everywhere.

Ugliness.

We are at a moment in our shared history when I likely do not even need to define the ugliness. We see, hear and experience varying degrees of it daily. Everything is political. Everything is an argument. People are living in various stages of fear, anger and suspicion toward one another. Various groups regard the medical community, scientists, police, media and more with contempt, anger and dismissal—and the contempt is loud and troubling. As economies decline and nations become unstable, there is an inevitable sense that life as we've known it is beginning to slip away, and there is absolutely nothing we can do about it. There was a time in which I mourned the passing of civility, manners and kindness to strangers. We once mourned the death of civil debate and honorable disagreement. Today, we wonder at the loss of rationality and competence in our civic leaders. Tomorrow, we will wonder when the lawlessness will spread to our city and what it means to be at peace.

The question arises, "How did our world get so ugly, dark and brutal?" There is the ugliness that we can see clearly now, but the underlying elements of darkness that fuel the external ugliness are even more troubling. There are ideas, values and dark perspectives that are working behind the scenes, shaping people's thoughts and desperate actions. People do not listen to one another, nor do they reason together in disagreement, because they have no sense of the worth or dignity of the person they are disagreeing with. Indeed, the worst characterizations are applied to ideological enemies. They are not just wrong; in the modern expression of merciless rage at our ideological enemies, they are *Nazis, white supremacists, racists.* They are characterized as *fascists, liars, corrupt rats* and *absolutely and irredeemably evil.* Once these designations are applied, there can be no mercy, no redemption, no reconciliation. Anything people do to keep this kind of evil, useless person out of any kind of power or influence seems justifiable. If your ideological enemy is, in your mind, a Nazi or a white supremacist oppressor, then any means used to oppose that enemy could be considered righteous and noble.

This ugliness toward one another is, therefore, the fruit of dehumanizing the "other." In our zeal to keep the other side from obtaining power that threatens our way of life and the world as we want it to be, we have removed the beauty, dignity and humanity our Father in heaven has bestowed on other "image bearers"—those who were created in the image of Yahweh—before they were even born. This cultural moment has far more troubling consequences that will follow. Once we dehumanize our enemies this way, we begin to treat them accordingly, until we ultimately expel them altogether. We have arrived at a stage in history in which our humanistic attempts to make the world beautiful or preserve it equals the need to expel those whom we perceive as destroying our world. Presently, expulsion looks like the silencing of what we deem as harmful or destructive voices, effectively ending their ability to contribute to societal discourse. Ultimately, in the days to come, the removal of those whom the masses determine to be harmful or destructive will involve much darker, evil, brutal expressions of self-righteous justice, without due process or mercy.

When we believe these things about one another and begin to act on what we believe, the logical end of such ideas and values is an ugliness far, far beyond what we have seen up to now.

Our instinct in times such as these is fight or flight—we either try to fight or try to escape. We might fight to change or preserve our immediate context and forge the kind of life we want to live. Or we might disconnect, check out, tune out the noise and ignore the roar of the world around us as it rages and burns. The goal of this book, however, is to help us lay hold of a righteous way forward, a way that can empower us to bear long with the world we have been born into. There is a faith we can lay hold of that can empower us to endure with great hope. Such a faith empowers us to impact the world around us today in powerful ways, and to live joyfully free of the cares of this life that threaten to choke our hearts and extinguish the flame of our love for Jesus. There is a way forward in enduring and even conquering the ugliness around us by journeying deep into the beauty of God.

This is not a book about ugliness. Again, this is a book about beauty.

Beauty is a central feature of a vibrant life in God. It is the essential component of a sustained and enjoyable prayer life. It is at the core of human pleasure, wonder and delight. The beauty of God moves the awakened heart and fuels purity and holiness. Why? The dull, callused, bored heart was made for pleasure and will actively seek it out somewhere. We long to be occupied and engaged, and will therefore settle into the rut of far lesser pleasures than the eternal ones we were made to enjoy. Yet God made us to be preoccupied with the heights of ultimate beauty—the kind of beauty that fully thrills the heart and never, ever grows old, wearisome or boring. The limitless beauty of God is the only fuel for hearts aching for life, joy and pleasure that becomes increasingly more pleasurable. We have been invited through the Gospel and the work of the cross to drink deeply of the radiant, beautiful glory that we have entered into through Christ.

How God Conquers the Human Heart

Beauty is how God conquers the human heart. This is a new idea for many Christians. Beauty is not often presented as a subject central to our faith. It can therefore be strange to hear that beauty is an essential element of walking in holiness, experiencing the love of God and growing in our relationship with Him. The central feature, however, of our hope in God's promises to come is that He will make all things beautiful in His time. Solomon talks about this in Ecclesiastes 3:11, saying that God will make all things beautiful, and when He does, as the psalmist declared, Yahweh will adorn (clothe) Himself with that beauty and splendor (see Psalm 104:1–2).

The very proof that God is beautiful in character and nature—a beauty that He will put on display for all to see—is when we, His image bearers, are transformed to express that same beauty and splendor. This is the central premise of this book. The beautiful God is going to make you and me beautiful, along with His entire Church, before transforming this world and bringing it into the fullness of beauty. His people and this world, transformed into His idea of beauty without sin or corruption, will be God's "beauty résumé" by which He will fully conquer the hearts of all of humanity. Every knee will bow, and every tongue will confess that Jesus Christ is Lord, and that He is the only one worthy to rule over His created order.

Growing up in a Pentecostal church culture, I learned that experiencing God happened by experiencing the power of the Holy Spirit. I was taught to seek the experience of God's presence through a manifestation of the Spirit. Sometimes, this meant simply "feeling the presence of God," as Smith Wigglesworth and other Pentecostal heroes of the faith had done before me. This could mean a weighty presence of the Spirit that bore down on me, or an electric sense of the nearness of God in a manifest way. Historic Pentecostal renewals spoke of even more intense manifestations of God's presence that could cause physical manifestations like shaking, weeping, laughing or shouting. As a young man, I was therefore taught to "wait on the Lord" and seek the manifestations of His presence that might follow His "arrival" into a meeting.

I was also taught to operate in the gifts of the Spirit, or to engage when others "flowed" with the Spirit through the gifts. Body life meant that Christians could and should prophesy, heal the sick and cast out devils. The power of the Spirit expressed through the Body in ministering to one another is a powerful way of engaging with the wonder and awe of who God is and how He moves in our midst. This book is not a denial of these very powerful means of engaging with who God is. This was what my Christianity looked like in my formative years, and because of that, I grew to love the power and presence of the Holy Spirit in my life and in His Church.

Early on, however, I found that I did not know what to do in the meantime, while I waited for God to move. I could serve, work and play, but I felt as if something was missing from my pursuit of Jesus. I had an aptitude for apologetics and the pursuit of truth, which included an ability to expose flawed arguments. Unsurprisingly, my ability to win biblical arguments and advocate for biblical wisdom bore very little fruit in the teenagers and young adults I was ministering to at that time.

One could contend that this is true, by and large, for the Church of the Western world as well. The evangelical posture of defending the faith has fashioned Christian apologists who love truth and love exposing lies and deceptions, and who rightly seek to "hold fast what is good" (1 Thessalonians 5:21). However, the evangelical use of rhetoric, logic and appeals to reason has made little impact on the surrounding culture. I made little impact that way on my city and on the young people I was serving.

I love the power of the Holy Spirit and the manifestation of His presence. I love truth and appreciate the valuable tools available to me to defend truth and expose deception. Reason and logic have limitations, however, engaging the mind but often leaving the heart untouched and unmoved. The power of the Holy Spirit is a critical element of my faith, and the awe and wonder that God's power elicits go further than reason and logic in moving my heart. There is a reason that Pentecostal Christianity is the fastest growing expression of Christianity on the earth, and has been for the last century. The power of the Spirit was meant for a higher purpose, however, and not as an end in itself.

The Spirit's power can shock and awe us, but not sustain or fashion our hearts to be anchored and steady in every season. The power of God can capture our attention and excite our holy imagination, stirring us with genuine excitement to pursue God. The purpose of that power, however, is to point us toward His beauty.

It is God's beauty that awakens and moves our hearts before making them tender and responsive to God's truth and active leadership. Power commands attention. Once God has our attention, He wants to fasten our lives to His truth. The way He steadies and sustains us with His truth is through the delight and true joy we find in the revelation of His beauty. This book is an examination of how this works in our lives today, and where beauty is taking all of us before the Lord returns.

The Ultimate Way God Draws Us In

Beauty is the ultimate way God draws us into wholehearted love. What does the Bible mean when it references God's beauty? The words *beauty* and *beautiful* occur in the Old Testament over one hundred times, with many different ancient Hebrew words being used to express the idea of beauty at the core of God's being and desire.

The earth and the Garden where humanity was born were beautiful. *Eden* means paradise on earth. Therefore, one of our greatest longings from our inception is to return to that place of beauty as our eternal home with God. That there is beauty to enjoy—splendor, grandeur, brightness—is because beauty began as God's idea. His throne room is filled with light, colors, sounds, fragrance and beyond. Beauty is that which is pleasing to the senses, at times overwhelming them with splendor and grandeur. Our God, the Maker of heaven and earth, is the very source and ultimate definition of beauty.

The way God designed us makes us very responsive to beauty. Our senses are attracted or drawn to beauty because we were meant to become what we behold. As we are drawn to and then behold the ultimate beauty that God Himself displays and expresses, we are transformed to reflect that beauty ourselves. The apostle Paul wrote about this: "But we all, with unveiled face, beholding as in a mirror the glory of the Lord, are being transformed into the same image from glory to glory, just as by the Spirit of the Lord" (2 Corinthians 3:18). Seeing aspects of God's infinite splendor and beauty has a powerful transforming impact on our lives. God subdues and conquers the hearts of His people simply by letting them see small glimpses of Himself. Our minds are renewed by something more than knowing what God wants; they are washed and made new (beautiful) by knowing what God is like. Knowing His thoughts, emotions, attributes and character forms our thinking in very powerful ways.

At the very beginning, God made the earth beautiful. It was pleasing to behold and dwell in, and its trees were "pleasant to the sight and good for food" (Genesis 2:9). In other words, God was neither utilitarian nor sparse in creating this world for humanity to dwell in. In one simple phrase describing the origins of the earth, we learn that God desired that our world be pleasant, and that beauty excite all our senses. He desired that what we see would be pleasant, while at the same time being pleasing to eat as well. Flavor and taste are part of the plan of beauty God conceived in crafting a place for us to dwell with Him forever.

That humanity was set within the Garden surrounded by powerful rivers means that fragrance was also part of what God intended for the paradisiacal context He set us into. Moses wrote that humanity was formed from the dust in the wilderness, and then was set within the Garden of perfection. From this context of ultimate beauty, where Adam and Eve communed with the Maker of heaven and earth, the very source and definition Himself of beauty, humanity was given the mandate to govern and steward that beauty and expand it outward from Eden to tame and transform the wild world around them (see Genesis 1:28).

In other words, the very mission and mandate of humanity from the beginning was to both "tend and keep" the Garden, or to nurture beauty (Genesis 2:15). It was also to expand it beyond Eden, or to make all things beautiful beyond the boundaries of Eden where humanity dwelt. The promise of God to make all things beautiful—declared by the prophet Isaiah, and again at the end of the book of Revelation—is about the restoration of the paradise He made and the beauty that He planted with His own hands, by which the earth becomes "new" again (see Isaiah 43:19; 65:17; Revelation 21:5).

The ones who were born to bear (express) God's image were meant to be the ones who partner with Him in this glorious mission to beautify the world. We clean, decorate and improve our homes, yards, gardens and workplaces because of the deep yearning of the human heart to both keep beauty and make beautiful. We are drawn to aesthetics—beautiful homes, beautiful places and spaces, even outwardly beautiful people. We have an interior drive to make ourselves and the spaces we inhabit beautiful. Beauty—both a love for it and a desire to express it—lies at the core of what makes us human.

In this book I also intend to explore the application of beauty from the Scriptures into our perseverance, interior transformation and ultimate destiny prior to the return of Jesus (and beyond). God has a plan to impart His beauty into His people and express that beauty to the world around us. Christianity built around our circumstances—how people treat us, how things work themselves out in our lives (or don't work out), how our money and honor land in comparison to those around us—is not an enduring, powerful or deep expression of faith and love for Jesus. Our self-centered interior orientation can fully turn outward, however, as beauty empowers us to set our love and trust completely on Him. His global "beauty plan" is designed to take our breath away, and in doing so, to set our hearts with resolve into the larger redemptive storyline unfolding around us. God reveals His beauty to stabilize our hearts, even as everything that can be shaken begins to shake.

This is the story of the Church, in all her glory and beauty—both presently and in the coming days. The Church doesn't seem to have a compelling story at the moment, whether in the eyes of a broader world that dismisses her or even within the Church itself. Those outside the Church, and often those inside, sometimes have a very low opinion of the broader Body of Christ in light of exposed sin and weakness. The Church seems very, very weak and very, very sinful. She does not seem beautiful to any who care to observe her. It seems impossible that she will be beautiful in the future.

This is, of course, a reflection of how we view ourselves personally. We don't feel as though we have a very compelling story as it relates to the global purposes and plans of God. We don't feel qualified to engage in the full glory and beauty of what God is going to do in the earth. We have a much more pronounced sense of our weakness and sin than we do of His love and emotions toward us. Yet God tells a very different story about us and those we love than the story that we perceive.

This is powerfully true about the Church as well. Whatever story the world or we ourselves tell about her, we can be confident that Jesus is telling a very different story about His Bride. At the same exact time, He is writing a very different story for her rapidly unfolding future and destiny—and it is a very, very beautiful story. He is going to impart His beauty into our lives and into His Church in fullness.

That is the power of beauty as God imparts it through grace. Beauty anchors us into Him, setting within us the necessary elements of an unshakable life. As our lives become rooted and grounded in His love and beauty, we become a powerful expression of who God is and what He is like. Our lives as His image bearers testify to the superiority of His leadership and His ways, drawing the hearts of the men and women around us to follow Him willingly (see Ephesians 3:16–19).

Beauty transforms, and beauty provokes. This is a critical process for each of us as individual followers of Jesus. It is also how God proves to the world that His Son is worthy to be the King of kings, Lord over all, Ruler of heaven and earth. Beauty experienced and expressed becomes the résumé of Jesus, by which every knee ultimately bows and every tongue confesses that He is Lord.

How does God do it? How does He help us willingly and freely love and obey Him, in full voluntary agreement with His leadership and will? How does He transform our hearts to be filled with mercy for the weak, the broken and the unsafe? He is unmatched in His ability to cause our hearts to freely choose to love, serve and bless our enemies who are set against us. What is the incredible process and journey into mature love that ends with us loving and serving His Church the way He does, even in the face of rage, resistance and trouble on every side? How does He set within us the kind of love and tenderness toward people that endures and transcends pain, disappointment and doubt?

He does all of this by leading us perfectly and skillfully in a manner that awakens and provokes us to choose His way of love, mercy, tenderness and generosity voluntarily. The way that He draws us—past our resistance, through our weakness and immaturity—into a love so different from the world's is with His beauty. As we shall see, beauty is the key to unlocking our full destiny in Christ.

Finally, this book will be an exploration of our process and journey as image bearers of God's beauty. We will explore the brilliance of the Lord's wisdom and leadership in our lives. The fullness of our hope rests in His ability to bring us into our destiny and calling in Him, as we endure faithfully and grow in love. The beauty of the Lord is something that He desires—with great zeal—to impart into our lives. Our beautiful God is passionate about beautifying His creation. All that humanity has corrupted or defiled will be made new. All things will be made beautiful. The wonder of His plan to make all things beautiful is that He begins right here, right now, with you and me.

PART ONE

OUR JOURNEY INTO GOD'S BEAUTY

Beauty That
Reorients Our Life

What is your life oriented toward? There are basic desires that orient our lives and drive our actions and choices. At a base level, we want our material needs met—food, clothing, a home and the means or resources to provide these necessities. In the process of acquiring the resources necessary to build our lives, we also have emotional and relational needs that must be met. Our Creator declared in the Garden of our origination: "It is not good that man should be alone" (Genesis 2:18). We need companionship, friendship and acceptance from those around us. We were created with a need for unconditional acceptance—to be loved and cherished despite our weaknesses and shortcomings. While our material needs might be met on an ongoing basis, if our emotional needs are not met, our relationships will become toxic and unmanageable and our behaviors even more broken and unhealthy.

Beyond these base material and emotional needs, we have desires and longings in the depths of our souls that were placed there by our Father. Some of these desires include a longing for greatness and impact, or a life of genuine significance. Our desire to be loved runs deeper than we realize, too, beyond the surface friendships and small talk that fills our lives. We long to be enjoyed, and to experience the beauty of intimacy without shame. We also have a profound desire to be wholehearted, or fully given to the people and things we love. Finally, we were made for pleasure, and we have a deep desire to be fascinated or captivated by beauty.

A fulfilling and ultimately satisfying life therefore looks like one in which we are known and enjoyed freely, just as we are right now, in all our weaknesses and deficiencies. We want to engage at a deep relational level with the ones whom we trust and feel safe with, genuinely connecting and being known and understood. We want to make genuine contributions that serve those around us who care about us, and we want to have a lasting impact long after we have gone. We want to be fully engaged with all our hearts into these kinds of relationships and significant, meaningful contributions. In the process, we want to be fascinated by beauty along the way.

By design, our deeper needs and longings ultimately find their greatest fulfillment and satisfaction when met by God Himself. His desire is to capture our hearts and fascinate us with His beauty, as the one who authored all beauty. His very design of the human spirit works in us to define beauty. The elements of style, color, design and order that people draw from to determine what is beautiful originated within Him.

It is God Himself who ultimately "satisfies the requirements" of aesthetic or external beauty as a means of drawing us into an exhilarating relationship with Him. This relationship reveals to us the far more profound beauty of His personality, emotions and character. His beauty is inextricably linked to His love—specifically, to how He loves in a manner that brings powerful and eternal resolution to our human search for acceptance and understanding, without shame or rejection. There is no one who loves us like the One who knows us deepest and best.

This kind of beauty awakens and stirs our hearts, and this kind of love frees and empowers our hearts with the kind of fearless, courageous engagement with God that we were made to express. This is the kind of love that ignites the wholehearted response we long to give. We don't want to hold anything back or live a safe, risk-free life when we feel secure in love. We want to be fully given and are therefore positioned by Jesus' love to make the kind of significant, long-term impact that we have quietly and desperately been wanting to make on the world around us. This is the kind of life God wants for us—one of significance, fulfillment and purpose from a place of confident rest, as we experience the pleasure of being loved and enjoyed by God and others whom we serve and bless.

Pursuing and growing into this kind of life takes a significant, long-term reorientation of our hearts. Between our own sinfulness or fallenness and the fallen world we have been raised in, we have learned to order our lives around the absence of God rather than around His dynamic presence in our lives. In His relative absence in our thinking and daily experience, our value systems and priorities have been ordered around the satisfaction of our material and emotional needs, with ourselves as the primary source we draw from.

In addition, we have learned to draw from one another for significance, satisfaction and strength. Both sources—ourselves and other people—are profoundly limited, broken, toxic and ultimately dissatisfying and disappointing. Men and women fail one another, fail themselves and even at their best use and exhaust one another in seeking to satisfy the never-ending search for fulfillment and pleasure.

The current orientation of many people's hearts is built around unhealthy compulsions and unsatisfied desires. Our culture defines success according to the social and economic systems that reward us with honor, privilege, affirmation, increased resources, finances and influence. In other words, we learn to define success according to the measure in which our material needs are assured and our emotional and relational needs are satisfied in relationship with our material needs. If people like us and reward us in ways that contribute to our financial and material stability, we feel a sense of professional fulfillment and personal satisfaction. All of this builds within our souls a love of money and a loyalty to it that supersedes all other loyalties. Our emotional and relational needs therefore become subservient to our need for material security, rather than being complementary to it. All of our needs and desires—material, emotional, relational—need to be met in a manner that helps us feel safe and secure. Otherwise, our resultant insecurity positions us to be adversarial to the people who threaten our sense of well-being.

Unless God is our source and supply, the one who meets our deepest needs and desires in the way that best satisfies our hearts, we will never be at rest. We will never, ever be free.

The First and Great Commandment

In the gospels, Jesus sums up the entirety of the Law of Moses in one command. In doing so, He gives us the essence of Christianity and the ultimate statement of what it is that our heavenly Father wants to produce in our lives. In one command, all of humanity is given the "measuring rod" that redefines what truly matters. Life, success and significance must now be defined by our ability to love God.

In the Law of Moses, the command to Israel was to "love the LORD your God with all your heart, with all your soul, and with all your strength" (Deuteronomy 6:5). In the gospel of Matthew, Jesus declares, "You shall love the LORD your God with all your heart, with all your soul, and with all your mind" (Matthew 22:37). In the gospels of Mark and Luke, Jesus states that we shall love the Lord our God with all our heart, soul, mind and strength (see Mark 12:30; Luke 10:27). In each gospel, Jesus follows His initial declaration with the command to "love your neighbor as yourself." He both summarizes Yahweh's command, given through Moses, to love God by keeping

His charge, statutes, judgments and commandments (see Deuteronomy 11:1), and He makes a critically important point—one that defines our lives and shapes our destinies. The point is this: Apart from obeying His commands, it is impossible to fulfill the commandment to love God. His commands serve the express purpose of directing our lives toward loving the people around us. It is therefore impossible to succeed at loving God wholeheartedly without loving the people around us who populate our lives.

Jesus added another key point to this commandment when He established it as "the *first* and *great* commandment" (Matthew 22:38, emphasis added). This commandment is to be understood as the one that takes highest priority as the Holy Spirit works in our lives, since love for God is the primary thing the Spirit wants to bring forth in us by grace and the work of His power. This new, highest of priorities now goes beyond redefining success; it establishes our life purpose and essential meaning. If work, family life, material goods and even ministry itself (and ministries themselves) do not contribute to, promote and in some way help produce a life flowing with love for Jesus in every measure of our heart, our soul, our thoughts and our time, energy and money, then those pursuits are essentially meaningless. We are answerable at the Judgment Seat of Christ related to this one measurement of our lives: Did we truly love God, and did our love for God involve loving others?

This is the "great" commandment in that it is the one most beneficial for our lives and future. It is first in priority and importance, and great in scope and impact. It encompasses everything pertaining to life and godliness, defining, but also permeating and fundamentally reshaping, our very quality of life and how we experience and enjoy it. To be reoriented and recalibrated to Jesus' value system and definition of success is to begin to touch the deepest places of desire and satisfaction, of fulfillment and reward. To engage in the first and great commandment is to answer the issues and compulsions of the heart, making our spirituality practical and achievable daily.

Jesus' command brings meaning to the mundane, small and unexciting areas of our lives. It brings dignity and beauty through dynamic purpose and fulfillment found in hidden places, unnoticed and overlooked by most people, and unappreciated by those who seek to reward us according to a very empty, meaningless societal system. Now it is possible for every stay-at-home parent, every accountant, teacher, insurance specialist and beyond to excel in the Kingdom and be great in the sight of the Lord, regardless of who notices, rewards or affirms it. A great reward awaits a very different kind of hidden life, small and unimportant in the eyes of others. We can live beautiful lives filled with genuine, sincere love for Jesus. We can overcome pain, rejection and offense to love as He loves. We can know that it means something related to our future to make these kinds of difficult choices. We can now live before an audience of One, laboring by grace to offer Him our thought life, our personality, our passions and emotions, and our personal resources as a daily offering of love to Him who satisfies all our longings.

What else could so beautifully define our lives? What else could give us dignity, strength and purpose in a manner that enables us to make every minute count for something eternal that is outside the societal pressure to produce and achieve?

A Prayer Life That Beautifies Our Hearts

The difficulty Christians have in laying hold of this new measurement for success is that it comes with a high initial cost. It is not easy to redirect our heart, soul, mind and strength toward something that initially seems to have little immediate benefit for our bank account and reputation. It is never easy to pass up the chance to seize an opportunity or stand out amongst the crowd. It is never easy to serve and invest in others without caring about what they offer us in return. Social rules ingrained over the course of our lives have conditioned us to care about the immediate, temporal rewards we can get from the people around us who most seem to impact the quality of our lives.

To truly embrace the first and great commandment and make it the central pillar of what our lives are about therefore requires an inward transformation. This will change how we think, what we care about, how we feel about the small transactions of love that no one else sees or appreciates, and ultimately what we give our time and energy to. In other words, to succeed at this commandment is to be radically transformed in our mind, soul and heart, which changes the way we give our strength.

Of course, we cannot simply decide to change the very core of who we are, what we value and how we think. It takes more than time and effort. It takes a genuine work of grace, by the power of the Holy Spirit working within us. This kind of transformative grace happens as we recognize the truth of God's Word and our need to align our hearts and lives to what He cares about, followed by genuine repentance that involves turning to God for help to change inwardly. Only He can transform us from within; we cannot change ourselves.

God must be the initiator and source of what is right and true, along with providing the power for us to walk in His truth. He instructs and helps us since we are powerless to understand and obey without the activity of the Holy Spirit in our lives as the Helper (John 14:26; 15:26; 16:7). Love for Jesus in us flows from the Spirit. As we are loved, we are "washed by His love" and empowered to love Him back. Therefore, it is impossible to grow in love for Jesus without talking with Him from His Word on a continual basis.

Let me explain. As I spent the last few decades working in a prayer ministry, I discovered the beauty of God-centered, scriptural prayers that ask for help from a place of growing confidence in who God is and what He wants to impart. These kinds of prayers are not "better" than other types of prayers. I am not submitting the idea that these are the prayers God enjoys more. Every moment we spend reaching toward our Father who loves us is a moment very well spent. Every small reach moves the heart of God and contributes to our life with Him. The benefit of God-centered, scriptural prayers is in their power to move *our own hearts*, not the heart of God.

That is the divine logic of why the prayers of the New Testament are worded in the manner that they are. They are designed to accelerate the movement of our hearts and capture us with the beauty of who God is, what He is like and what He wants to impart to His people. Praying the prayers of Scripture is one of the gifts God has given us to help us. His prayers, His Word and His commands are all for our benefit and help. God therefore connects our loving Him with our prayer and obedience, or our connection and agreement with Him. As we yield our own strength and ways and turn ourselves to access His power, help and wisdom, our heart, soul, mind and strength are all transformed over time as we grow in love for Him.

The redefinition of our lives around love—love from Jesus, love for Jesus—changes everything. It happens very slowly, over a long period of time, as we faithfully chip away at the orientation of our soul around this world's value systems and rewards. Over time, through prayer, diligent study of God's Word, and the continual work of the Holy Spirit in our lives, the "spirit of wisdom and revelation" that Paul prayed we would experience slowly imparts experiential truth and clarity to us about the Word and heart of God (Ephesians 1:17).

As we reach out to connect continually with Jesus over many years, the cumulative impact of tens of thousands of small encounters with His Holy Spirit and truth transforms our perspective and our sense of what matters. These are the small but significant moments that we don't count as "God encounters," but they constitute the many—almost imperceptible—ways that God transforms our thinking and emotions over time. It may be that you are listening to a sermon, the content of which you have heard many times before. It may be that as a Scripture is explained, suddenly it feels as if you have never heard of that verse before and it is striking your holy imagination for the first time. In that moment, the Word of God, some key ideas, some perspectives and truths about Jesus and how He thinks and feels—suddenly, it just makes sense to you. It clicks, and suddenly you think differently about your situation, about God, about your future or about your friends and family.

As we make loving God our primary ambition, the re-orientation of our soul causes us to reach for and become students of His love. There are dozens and dozens of varied expressions of Jesus' love in Scripture, but our inward, self-focused orientation can make us miss so many of the ways that Jesus expresses His active love for us daily. We do not have an eye for His beauty and therefore miss the details of His love. Our prayer lives are far more focused on our own deficiencies than they are on His sufficiency.

However, as we begin to pray and ask God to reveal Himself to us, to show us who He really is and what He is really like—and most powerfully, to give us a greater understanding of how He loves us—He will answer us in small but very significant ways. Slowly, suddenly, the eyes of our understanding are enlightened and we see details that we can comprehend and apply into our specific situations (see Ephesians 1:18–19). We whisper to Him, *This is how You feel about me, right here, today. . . .*

The truth connects and begins to take root in our heart. We begin to believe that what we are perceiving is real, and true, and beginning to redefine and reshape our lives.

2

Beauty That Redefines Success and Greatness

As we begin to perceive, comprehend and believe that Jesus loves us in the specific ways that Scripture and the grace and power of the Holy Spirit reveal to us, our hearts and lives begin to stabilize. We begin to grow in genuine confidence in the love of Jesus and feel secure in our relationship with Him. We begin to believe that His love and commitment are far greater and stronger than our weakness and areas of compromise.

This interior stability unlocks our destiny. Suddenly, we have the genuine power from within—combined with the profound tenderness and compassion—to truly begin to love those around us with the same quality of love Jesus has expressed toward us. We have the power to obey God with a free heart and genuinely please Him as we express love for Him and for others. Obedience to God involves more than staying within set boundaries as we avoid sin and those things that are contemptible and destructive. Obedience to God also is about the quality and consistency of our love and service to others as we seek to abide in Christ daily.

Jesus stated it plainly: Loving God involves obedience to God. Jesus did not make obedience mysterious. In His teaching and preaching, He gave us a clear way forward in obedience to Him that provides us with some specifics about how we walk out the first and great commandment. In the glory and beauty of His wisdom, He establishes this commandment as the top priority in our lives, and then He connects our obedience to fulfilling it. Finally, we discover that our obedience to God has profound benefits in our interior transformation and growth into mature love for Him.

In other words, by setting our hearts to love God, we subsequently seek to obey Him. As we lay hold of the grace and power to obey Him, that obedience accelerates our transformation and empowers us to grow in love and affection for Him. Jesus commands us to love God and gives us the details of what that love looks like in obedience. That obedience becomes the means that empowers us to do the thing He commanded us to do.

The first and great commandment is therefore more than a command to obey; it is a prophecy about our future that Jesus is confident He can deliver us into. He declares, "You *shall* love the Lord your God." The reorientation of our hearts around the pursuit of His love is the beginning stage of the "beautification" of our lives. This reorientation happens through the beauty of God's grace at work in our lives. It continues as we partner and cooperate with that grace. We want to be settled in our identity as ones loved by God and find our greatest success and fulfillment in loving Him back. This takes the slow and steady realignment of our thinking to agree with Jesus in what He thinks about us, how He feels about our obedience and what life is truly about from His perspective.

A New Definition of Greatness

In His Sermon on the Mount, Jesus addressed many of our core needs and provided a framework for what reorientation should look like for the follower of Christ (see Matthew 5–7; Luke 6:20–49). Jesus revealed to us in this sermon what a transformed heart that loves Him looks like, and how obedience contributes to that transformed heart. The Beatitudes He gave us in Matthew 5 are a new definition of greatness. They provide the very definition of a beautiful heart that reflects who the Father is. These values and attitudes express His own heart and the way He expresses His love for people. The attitudes of the heart that God desires to produce in us through grace are therefore reflected in these Kingdom values that Jesus established as our top priority. Walking out the first and great commandment is only possible when we seek to embody the Beatitudes and obey the commands that follow them in this sermon. These Beatitudes include poverty of spirit, mourning, meekness, hungering and thirsting for righteousness, mercy, purity of heart, peacemaking and enduring persecution for the sake of the Gospel.

If we think about our heart as a garden we are to care for, tend and nurture, the Beatitudes of Christ would be the primary flowers that the Father wants to see grow there. The entire sermon is a practical instruction for every Christian on how to grow our heart in these specific ways. Jesus identifies the toxins (sinful areas of the heart) that poison the garden, and these we must recognize honestly with humility, and deal with ruthlessly. He gives us the key lifestyle practices that nurture and cultivate a life flowing in the heart attitudes we are growing in. He then helps us understand and navigate the often frustrating and painful relational dynamics that accompany a life oriented around the Beatitudes. Finally, He gives us as His people a clear vision for why we want to go on the long and difficult journey to lay hold of heart attitudes that are foreign—and even hostile—to the normal human internal orientation and external social expression.

The cultivation of the Beatitudes is how we express our love back to Jesus over our lifetime. They are also the primary way that Jesus defined the successful collective impact of His Church as we engage society together. How does this work? The answer Jesus gave is the central idea of this book. He describes impact in a way very different from the social activism that constitutes the normal means by which people seek to bring about change in our modern world. Jesus gave us a template for genuine societal changes—powerful, deep, comprehensive changes that involve justice, righteousness and peace. External impact begins with internal transformation. Jesus used the imagery of salt that preserves and light that reveals to illustrate the way the Church would impact society through the

Beatitudes (see Matthew 5:13–16). This imagery indicates that His priority for His people is personal transformation that many of us will express together in a manner that profoundly testifies to the superiority of His ways and His Gospel.

Jesus' plan seems impossible—millions and millions of Christians prioritizing the first and great commandment and cultivating the Beatitudes together around the world. Millions and millions of Christians transformed from within by grace, growing in and expressing authentic love for Jesus on His terms, as a powerful display of His beauty to the earth. Understanding this helps us understand Jesus' commitment to the Church and the necessity of New Testament–based communities that engage in living out the Sermon on the Mount together.

Jesus' intention and plan is to put something on display that will shock the world. We know why the world will be shocked. The Church is currently under fire in various places around the globe. She is being dismissed and diminished, forsaken, persecuted and broken, and she is often guilty of genuine abuses and sins that threaten to disqualify her witness of the Gospel to the nations she serves. The weak, broken and sinful humanity of the Church is currently on full display for all to see. The narrative attached to the Church and the Scriptures that undergird her is unflattering and troubling.

The Church in various places—to various degrees—seems currently prayerless, powerless and helpless to intervene and stop the cultural decline of the West. More pointedly, the "reorientation" of our hearts to the Gospel, to align our lives around the first and great commandment and the Sermon on the Mount, doesn't seem to have taken root with the Body of Christ worldwide. The things that millions of churches worldwide are supposed to embody and express together seemingly are not being embraced or understood. The things that bring condemnation and shame to the Church seem to be driving the cultural conversation about her.

Ultimately, even we as the Church don't believe that the Lord could or would do anything close to what the Bible describes. Quietly, we believe many of the world's narratives and critiques of the Church. We don't have the faith to believe that it's possible that Christians from around the world, from every denomination, will collectively express the Beatitudes and live the Sermon on the Mount in full unity and maturity.

Yet the Father will do all of this in and through His people, and much, much more. The Lord will turn everything around through His skillful leadership and patient lovingkindness, without violating the free will of any of His saints to force them to embrace His leadership. This single act of sovereign beauty, expressed through the weakest and most unimpressive of peoples, will set the entire world on fire. It will be the single most powerful statement ever made about who He really is.

Our "Mustard Seed God" is joyfully committed to turning this negative storyline of a weak, broken and sinful Church upside down with every Christian who wants to know and love Him around the world (see Matthew 13:31–32). That the current expression of what He wants the Church to be in fullness is very, very small does not trouble Him. Jesus loses no sleep over the condition of

His Bride. He has a much larger narrative, with a clearer perspective about her and how she is doing. In fact, He is not even mostly concerned with how His Bride is doing; He is primarily committed to where she is going. He is confident in His plan and leadership, and therefore is not upset about the "smallness" of the Church currently related to the first and great commandment, the Sermon on the Mount and the global impact she is having.

While it is helpful to hear that this is where it's all going, it is far more important to respond and ask the Lord to begin with us. We do not have to—nor should we want to—wait for the future to reorient our lives around the commandment He gave us and the values He set for us in the Sermon on the Mount. We can and must begin today. We can reach for the grace of God that is available to us to align our thoughts, values and idea of success with the Father's heart. This is the kind of life God wants us to live; therefore, He will help and empower us to do so. We don't have to will our way into these heart attitudes. We surrender our way, and repent our way, into the will of God for our life. When we yield our thinking and realign it to agree with His way forward for us, great power comes from Him that will transform us and beautify our hearts to move like His heart.

A New Life Vision: Wholehearted Pursuit

In the very beginning of the Song of Solomon, the young Shulamite bride expresses a critically important vow to her bridegroom: "Draw me away! We will run after you" (Song of Solomon 1:4). This request expresses our greatest need and desire as the Bride of Christ to be drawn by the Holy Spirit's power deep within our hearts into intimacy with God, coming close to the Father's heart. If we are drawn by God's love, our vow is to respond and pursue Him extravagantly in worship and loving obedience with our whole heart.

The reorientation of our lives cannot begin with a mere decision for Christ or our own resolve to be a better Christian. We cannot draw from within ourselves to become the kind of Christian we want to be. The reorientation of our lives around God's definition of greatness, around what He declares is valuable and important, must begin with His incomparable beauty and extravagant love for us. We must be captured by His beauty. We must experience His love. Our aim and highest goal in life must be to grow continually in that experience so that we might experience more of His love and beauty.

The reason this journey does not begin from within is that our starting point in wanting to love God well is broken. Our love is often mixed with shame, condemnation and inadequacy, which keep us at a distance from Jesus. Or our love is lukewarm and is mixed with lethargy and dullness. Our brokenness and sinfulness mean that we have little to nothing to draw from on the inside to muster up passion for Jesus. Our life vision—a vision that understands that success is rooted in the love of God—must therefore see Jesus as the author, initiator and finisher of our faith. Love *for* Jesus starts with love *from* Jesus.

We need a secret history in God that begins with the sweet work of His love to awaken, stir and move our cold hearts. Our life in God starts with God. If we are stuck until He helps us, and if we understand that the primary issues of life are all connected to His help, we will set our hearts differently. Rather than trying to find the inner resolve to change ourselves and present ourselves to Him as willing, holy vessels, we channel our resolve into reaching for His grace, power and love that change us. I believe the Father's greatest desire is to present us to Jesus as a finished product, a Bride loved and powerfully prepared for the day of the gladness of His heart. It is the Father's joy to love us into loving Him back, and to love us into loving His Son and the people around us the way He loves them.

Love flows from the Father to us, and as we experience it, we begin to love Him back. When we love Him back, He expresses love back to us again as we build our history with Him. This empowers us to love the people around us, eventually empowering us to love even those who are most difficult to love with a free and flowing heart, just as the Father did with us when our weak love began. This is a story about His beauty making us beautiful, and about the extravagant, overflowing affections of Christ causing our heart to flow deeply with His love.

Immersed in this kind of love, we can shift our life vision away from trying to make the best of it, trying to get through the day, trying to get to the top, or trying to be the best we can be. We can reorient our vision toward experiencing the fullness of beauty and love. This begins with a cry from the depths of our soul to be drawn by grace into profound fascination with Jesus and be filled with His love. Filled to overflowing, we can respond with an awakened resolve to run after Jesus in ministry and loving service to Him and to those around us. We *can* love Jesus with our whole heart. We *can* love others more than we are concerned with ourselves.

It begins with His beauty, and with the Lord's work to draw us away, into His love.

3

God Calls the Weak Ones Beautiful

It is intentional on my part to delay talking about what the Lord is going to do through the Church to impact the world in the future. It is of no value to talk about the Church's future, and about the vindication of God's name and reputation when she is transformed, if we secretly do not believe that *we ourselves* will be transformed or be part of a future, glorious destiny. One great obstacle that hinders us from walking in the fullness of life in Christ and the joy of our salvation is the presence of powerful arguments within our own souls against the beauty of the Gospel. The god we are most often serving is our own internal voice, deficient in the love of Jesus and His perspective on who we are and why we are valuable to Him. The inside voice we are enslaved to is the prideful voice of our own perfectionism and our own sense of failure and inadequacy.

Out of the many age groups I have served over the decades, I find that teenagers best articulate these internal arguments within us against the love of God and His Gospel. Teens might not yet grasp that layers of pride inside can exaggerate their failures, fuel their unbelief and measure their spiritual performance in ways foreign to the cross of Christ. But they somehow manage to simplify this mindset and interior struggle with their words. "Sure, I believe God loves me," they have told me over the years. "He has to. He's supposed to." Teens thus simplify love mostly to mean tolerance or acceptance, which speaks to one of the greatest felt needs any person has. People want to be accepted, not rejected, by those around them, even though they quietly do not truly tolerate themselves. While teenagers might resent their parents for loving them in ways that look like constant dissatisfaction and frustration with their imperfections, brokenness and immaturity, they also secretly agree that they are "lesser than" in comparison to others and do not have what it takes to succeed. The resulting anger isn't because they disagree with the criticisms of their parents and teachers. The anger comes from a desire not to be reminded again of the self-doubt they must live with every moment of every day.

I have found that this quiet anger in our young people, this secret desperation to escape the pain of their self-perception, follows them into marriage. Marital conflict is heightened because the nature of living with another person exaggerates the flaws and fault lines of brokenness and sin that is undealt with (and until marriage, is unperceived). We marry a mirror, reflecting back to us something more than the areas of brokenness we already secretly disliked or worked to ignore in ourselves. Marriage also forces us to reconcile our blind spots, the deficiencies and areas of brokenness we were unaware of prior to conflict with our spouse. We can hide our deficiencies from our co-workers and friends for a long time. In marriage, however, it is very difficult to hide for long, and the forced confrontations with the brokenness of our soul awaken greater measures of defensiveness, self-protection and heightened conflict.

It is no mystery, then, why young men retreat into the escape of games, mindless recreation and shallow conversation. They jostle for position and significance within their small social circles and find outlets for their interior anger, while hiding away from the pain of their inadequacy and hoping no one notices or calls attention to it. They rarely feel safe or enjoyed, and almost never feel truly free. They are friends with other young men, yet feel profoundly isolated and alone.

Young women are subject to the same interior torment, but they don't deal with it in the same way. I have found that while young men are drawn to other young men to escape the torment of their souls and their broken estimation of self, the internal torment of the soul works differently with many women. It drives them away from potential friendships with other women. Comparison and competition with other females, and internal dissatisfaction with themselves, lead many women to lose themselves in their work, their homes and their children. There are few safe places to express their profound frustrations and dissatisfaction with their spouse, beyond expressing them directly. Young women feel alone in the struggle to build a home because they are alone. A husband can provide very little actual help that will satisfy a young wife's unfulfillment and the helpless, powerless feeling that the ache of inadequacy and the pain of self-hatred spark within her soul. When she looks around at other families—whether it be leadership in the Church, her social media friends or women who inspire others—these offer a grim comparison between herself and those who seem to "have it all." She hopes that no one will see how little to nothing she has to boast about.

These descriptions sound like the lives of men or women who are not in the faith, not filled with the Holy Spirit and not liberated by the Gospel. Many decades of pastoral ministry have left me with the unfortunate observation, however, that many, many Christians are saved by grace, yet still live as if they are not. Their legal position spiritually might be eternally secured by faith in Christ, who justifies them, yet their living condition bears no resemblance to someone who has been apprehended by the extravagant love of Jesus.

The fact of our salvation is no guarantee of the quality of our new life in Christ. Salvation for many in a modern, Western context can offer different friends and a different sense of community than one might have had otherwise. It can also offer the possibility of help from other Christians when one is in need. Yet it also means trying to live up to an even higher standard than one had before, which can involve the greater expectations of others, coupled with a greater sense of shame at any failure to live up to the new social rules of one's spiritual community. The result can be a greater sense of loneliness and anger at what should be or could be, both within ourselves and within our Christian community, but often sadly is not.

Salvation through Christ in our modern context has been reduced to a mere prayer, or a decision or moment in which a person is apprehended by truth, with the promise of a relationship with a loving God. But then little to no means to have such a relationship is provided. Inspirational, skillful preaching with aspirational truths about God's love can bring momentary comfort, but very rarely does it bring interior transformation. A pastor can learn how to preach in a manner that keeps congregants engaged and in attendance. Yet many pastors I have spoken to over the years understand the delicate nature of their communal situation. So many of the listeners are looking for relief or escape from the interior frustrations and pain that their own undealt-with pride continually afflicts them with. We preach weekly in a manner that temporarily soothes but rarely heals their pain, leaving them without the internal "iron in the soul" that would enable them to endure the external pain that others inflict on them. Many saints wander endlessly as a result, hoping to find rest from their interior storm, yet rarely finding the elusive shelter that they seek. Many pastors therefore find themselves put in the position of serving faithfully as they navigate the continual movement of restless saints from place to place, church to church.

What God Feels for the Weak

What God feels for the weak ones, however, changes everything. The love Jesus wants us to understand, experience and therefore fully believe in is not restricted to the act of the cross. It is important to affirm that the cross is the ultimate and most beautiful expression of Jesus' love for us. Yet some reduce the cross to an ancient act of love for all of humanity in a manner that unwittingly depersonalizes their faith, stripping them of the revelation of God's daily affections and loving interactions with weak and broken saints.

God's love was powerful at the cross, and that same love is dynamically active today, seeking to penetrate our hearts. If we contemplate the cross alongside the daily interactions of a present, engaged God who desires active friendship with His people, we begin to embark on the kind of journey that truly does change our lives in every way. For many, the cross and the Gospel invitation are an introduction to a God they want to believe in, yet rarely progress to knowing intimately. There is so much more to the cross and what Jesus declared about humanity there, and there is so much more to how the same Man who was moved by love to embrace the cross centuries ago still feels about us today.

Jesus was motivated by love for us long before we were born. He was willing to give everything to secure eternal friendship with us. The secret to a transformed life begins with exploring the beauty of what moved—and still moves—Jesus' heart, both then and now. What is He thinking and feeling when He views our lives here and now? Our faith is unstable when we settle for projecting our own opinions and assumptions onto Him. The quiet desperation we live with is the fruit of our pride and the product of our insecurity. We must find an answer to our desperation, and that process begins outside our understanding, ultimately invading our thoughts and conquering them with beautiful truth. The mind of Christ and His thoughts and emotions toward us are mighty to tear down the fortresses we have built over time around our pain and dissatisfaction. As His truth—combined with the power of the Spirit to help us experience it—works to shift our thinking and perspective, our emotions stabilize, and our heart opens and begins to move and to feel again.

It is easy to believe that Jesus loves us if that belief incorporates the very narrow and ultimately impotent definition of love that means tolerance and acceptance. It is impossible to believe that Jesus loves us in the specific ways that the Bible describes. The narrative of Scripture describes Jesus as the true God who is fully Man, who also insists on intimate friendship with us, a friendship He secured through excruciatingly painful personal sacrifice. The Bible goes on to describe Jesus as the kind of faithful friend who is unfailingly loyal, impossibly merciful, incredibly patient and fully invested in His friendship with us. He loves us, and He also enjoys us. He likes us. He is interested in us. He is moved by our love for Him. He is responsive to it and is fully engaged in helping us grow to love Him back more fully. His love, emotions, desires and passions are filled with overflowing joy as He engages with us in our brokenness, sin and deficiencies. While we were yet sinners, Jesus died for us. While we are still immersed in the struggle to overcome that sin and brokenness, Jesus enjoys us and takes great pleasure in His relationship with us.

This kind of beautiful love is impossibly good news, and our pride refuses to believe it is real.

The Truth That Changes Everything

On one occasion, I was with a bunch of brothers in the faith whom I had just met. They are awesome guys, and I enjoy the times I now get to spend with them. This particular time, we were praying together. When I listened to their prayers, I was struck by a potential deficiency in the "diet" of the knowledge of God in their lives. If you do not consume enough iron or vitamin C or other specific nutrients in your daily diet, you will eventually have a problem. In the same way, there was a deficiency in these guys' theological diet that informed their prayer life.

This is true of me as well! I have my own theological deficiencies, which present their own challenges in my daily life. So I am not telling this story to expose my brothers, nor am I assuming that my prayer life is "better" than theirs. How we pray with, speak to, serve and engage one another in relationship and conflict is all a fruit of what we know and believe about God and the world He made—and our place in that world before Him.

Several of the guys took turns praying, and all their prayers expressed the same "reach" for the Lord's help in the same way: *Lord, I need to do this task. Lord, help me do this task. Lord, I want to do this task. I thank You that it's Your will that I accomplish this task.*

All of their prayers were a checklist of *I'm supposed to . . .* They were praying these requests passionately. They were not praying robotically or stoically. They were feeling it. They are God-fearing lovers of Jesus, reverent men of prayer, yet each one's prayer life in that moment was about *me* and what *I'm* supposed to do to please God. The entirety of their requests was therefore a plea for the Lord's involvement in their responsibilities: *God, I'm supposed to do this task . . . God, You know I need to do it, and I need to follow through and do it with excellence. God, I'm asking that You help me really do this task with excellence.*

It is important to stress again that these kinds of prayers are not bad, nor are they wrong. They are very common and may express your prayer life as you engage with the Lord. Again, I'm not looking to correct your prayer life— merely to add something significant to it that will change your heart and emotions toward God forever. In addition to our appeal to the Lord for His help, and our invitation for Him to enter into our world and our concerns (which, again, is beautiful prayer!), I want to suggest adding another element into our conversation with Jesus: *Lord, this is who You are. I love that You are like this. I'm asking that You do what You love to do in human hearts.*

When I pray, I want to talk with my dear friend, Jesus, whom I want to know as my God who is profoundly moved by my prayer. I want to talk about more than *me* and *my need*; I want to talk with God about *God*. I want to talk about what the Scriptures say that He wants to do and is really going to do. I want to ask Him, from His Word, to express the things that are in His heart here, in my world, amongst my friends and family.

The New Testament prayers of the apostle Paul and others can retrain us not to talk to God mostly about the deficiencies of His Church or our own deficiencies, but to talk to God mostly about God. As we reorient our hearts and lives around God's beauty, God's love and God's definition of success, our prayer lives will follow. Our prayer lives can become reoriented from self-focused and task-focused prayers to God-centered, biblical prayers—prayers we pray with affection and confidence that He enjoys us and our very small, weak reach to know Him.

Our prayers and our perspective—how we understand the world and our place in it—are a product of our theology. As my friends were praying, it became clear that they were coming from a paradigm of God that flows from *God, I want to please You.* That's beautiful. I find, however, that the reason the Gospel and the beauty of God in the Scriptures are so powerful is that they strengthen our paradigm of *God, I want to please You* by adding to it, *God, You are pleased with me.*

This is the part that so many Christians struggle with related to the good news of the love of Jesus. They believe in His love, yet they never begin to experience His beauty. They have a hard time believing that *God, You are pleased with me. You enjoy me right now. This is how You feel—it moves You so deeply that I am even praying at all, even for a moment. You love the sound of my voice and enjoy my weak little reach for You.*

With the Gospel and the revelation of God's beauty, my own Christianity eventually shifted from *God, I want to feel something* to being surprised by the truth of *God, You feel something.*

The apostle Paul wrote, "There is therefore now no condemnation to those who are in Christ Jesus, who do not walk according to the flesh, but according to the Spirit"

(Romans 8:1). The apostle John wrote, "To Him who loved us and washed us from our sins in His own blood, and has made us kings and priests to His God and Father" (Revelation 1:5–6). There is no rejection from the One who loved us and washed us in His own blood, lovingly cleansing us of that which separated us from His Father.

We could read the words of Paul in Romans and still argue with them, however, struggling with insecurity in our daily walk with Jesus. "No condemnation for those who do not walk according to the flesh?" we could argue. "I struggle with my flesh; therefore, I must be condemned!" Or we could decide, "At best, God loves me but is perpetually frustrated with my failures!"

Paul meets that argument against grace forcefully a few verses later: "But you are not in the flesh but in the Spirit, if indeed the Spirit of God dwells in you" (Romans 8:9). In other words, Paul is saying emphatically, *This is not who you are now! You have become something different—not because of what you have done, but because of what God has done. Therefore, if God has done it, He will now relate to you based on who and what you are now*. Paul is saying that you are a new creation in Christ (see 2 Corinthians 5:17). The God who set His Spirit inside you will not reject you, but will relate to you with fierce loyalty, unyielding commitment, extravagant lovingkindness, outrageous mercy and transcendent patience, without worry, fear or anxiety about your future.

When we begin to talk to God about who God is and what makes Him beautiful, we uncover and experience the detailed and incomparable fierceness by which He loves us. Little by little, His emotions and enjoyment, His delight and enthusiasm for our lives and future with Him begin to chip away at our unbelief and prideful protest. Our arguments falter. Our resistance fails. Slowly and patiently, His great love and enjoyment of us, even in our weakness, eventually conquer our fears and reset our hopes and dreams about what our lives with Him could become.

This truth from Scripture—that God enjoys us even when we are weak, or when we are broken and flawed—is critical for our future. We must know what God feels about us in our weakness and our brokenness. Why? We already know the truth about ourselves. Our lives, our ministries, our reach for God—all our spirituality and all our attempts to love Him back and love the ones around us in all the messiness—it is *all* weak. All our prayers and service, all our sincere efforts to be faithful to God and pleasing in His sight—*all* of it is small, weak and broken. To know that it still moves and delights Him, and that He enjoys every drop of it all and does not care at all about our opinion on the matter . . . changes everything.

The Beauty of a Stable Heart

Now, let's return to the beginning of this chapter. The truth that God enjoys us, even in our weak but sincere attempts to love Him back, changes how we feel about God, which then powerfully shifts how we feel about ourselves. Over time, if we steadily continue talking with God about these truths and His love and emotions toward us, if we feed our spirit with sermons and resources that fuel our understanding, and if we talk to others around us about these truths, we will feel our emotions change and our internal arguments settle down. Suddenly, the truth of God's Word and the reality of His love (specifically, what He thinks about us) become the far clearer "internal voice" we feel and hear as our emotions stabilize and our desires for God grow. We will begin to remember the days in which our pride exaggerated our sin and weakness while also distorting, diminishing or even dismissing His love for us.

The more we give time and attention to these truths and turn them into quiet conversation with the Lord, talking to God about God, the more these truths take root. The apostle Paul spoke about this in Ephesians 3:14–19:

> For this reason I bow my knees to the Father of our Lord Jesus Christ, from whom the whole family in heaven and earth is named, that He would grant you, according to the riches of His glory, to be strengthened with might through His Spirit in the inner man, that Christ may dwell in your hearts through faith; that you, being rooted and grounded in love, may be able to comprehend with all the saints what is the width and length and depth and height—to know the love of Christ which passes knowledge; that you may be filled with all the fullness of God.

The reorientation of our sense of self and how we are doing radically shifts as God slowly delivers us from the torment of our own opinions about our deficiencies, areas of sin and compromise, and pain related to self-hatred. The love of God teaches us how to love ourselves as He loves us. Slowly but powerfully, we begin to agree with God's version of our story and how He tells it. When my sense of what is true and real about me comes from God and not from within my own soul, I become less defensive, less sensitive to criticism, and more likely to stop hiding from the people around me as I become settled and at peace with who God says I am. The same will be true for you.

This kind of confidence in the love of Jesus in turn gives us confidence to love the people around us without fear of their rejection. To be, as Paul wrote in Ephesians 1:6, "accepted in the Beloved" is to grow into being unafraid of others rejecting us because of our deficiencies or inadequacies. Filled with confidence from Christ, our hearts are now able to be open, tender and filled with grace for others in their weakness. Our perspective about who people are radically changes, and suddenly our fear of the Lord is stronger than our fear of people.

Our love for the Lord is also stronger in us than the effects of other people's inability to love us back the way we might have previously felt we deserved. This is because we are growing into not relating with ourselves or others according to what we feel we deserve or they deserve. We remember our pride, our fear, our sense of powerlessness, pain and lonely isolation, and we are filled with gratitude for the God who loved us into a different journey with a very different end.

Fueled by gratitude, emboldened by love, kissed by mercy, we cannot help but be tender toward the weak ones around us in their sincere but broken attempts to navigate life and relate with us. Hopefully, we have not forgotten that we are still weak ones, too, on a journey into God's beauty, being made beautiful by His grace and love.

It starts with the simple act of a tender God, moved by our love, calling our weak but sincere broken life beautiful.

4

When the Brokenness of Others Fails Us

Our exploration of ultimate beauty and its power to bring us into our full destiny in Christ begins with Jesus and His love for us, but our journey ends with our hearts being filled with His love and faithful commitment to His Church. (By our journey ending here, I don't mean death. Death is not the end for the believer who is in Christ, although it does end our journey's earthly stage as we graduate into the next phase of God's eternal purposes for His people and the earth.) We can answer the question of what God has planned for our future with this simple premise—whatever the particulars of our occupation, our finances and our friends are, God's highest plan for our lives is to love our church and His Church the same way that He does. He is going to impart to us the same perspective, same loyalty and commitment, same patience, heart of mercy, tenderness and willingness to suffer long with weak, sinful and broken people as they embark on the very same journey we have been on.

This is, however, a challenging conclusion to a long and often very difficult journey. The victory of the cross and the power of the Holy Spirit will produce something breathtakingly beautiful in and through the people of God. Loving the Church—the whole Church—is a very difficult command for sincere believers who have been mishandled, mistreated, misunderstood and in some heartbreaking instances have had even worse sins committed against them by leaders, pastors and beyond. I have met many who are trying their hardest to forgive the Church and those in it who wounded them. I have met some others who have given up altogether and have distanced themselves with real fear that further pain awaits them if they reengage. I have worked with and worked through much with people whom I have wounded by my own poor leadership and immaturity. I have also helped people stabilize their hearts and lives after being impacted by the poor leadership of others.

It is not truly possible for you to get the most out of this book if we are stuck on this point of getting beyond being hurt by the Church. For some of us, trying to love the whole Church is a painful thorn that serves as a constant reminder of past conflicts, disappointments or even betrayals that still have real hooks into our heart and emotions. For many of us, there is a hesitation, a wariness and a difficulty to trust.

For others of us, the pain runs far deeper and the anger simmers just under the surface, ready to flow out at unexpected and even unwelcome moments that we aren't always ready to deal with. No matter how hard we try, we cannot get past or get over what was done—the injustice of it, and the way that real wrongs were committed and dismissed or diminished. In the process, we may have felt devalued, unimportant and eventually unwelcome. Thus, we had to pick up and start again elsewhere, but the damage was done.

I have met the most beautiful, sincere and faithful saints who still flinch and wrestle with the call to love a broken, immature and, at the worst of times and places, corrupt and abusive Church.

Heavenly Wisdom in the Face of Injustice

In my own country, a politically divided America, it was probably inevitable that the Church would become divided along similar lines. An observation I want to make is that one segment of the American Church expresses sincere love for the lost, while expressing genuine contempt for the (right-wing) Church. A very different segment seems to love the Church (or their "side" of it) more than they love the (left-wing) lost. Both sides seem fixated on the harm the other side can do to those whom they love.

There are, of course, more than two sides in opposition to one another, and there is contempt, pain, rejection or simply frustration leaving different Christians ready to write off entire large groups of other Christians within the global Church. These two sides I talk about, however, are a simple way of illustrating the dilemma of how difficult it is to love and fight for the whole Body of Christ. How can we move forward when both sides have dug in their heels, refusing to engage or hear the other side? In the face of injustice, the need for heavenly wisdom is greater than ever.

The core issue here—one that is still lacking in my own life—is a lack of tenderness and genuine mercy toward our enemies. Our "enemies" might include those who are wearying us with dogmatic self-righteousness. If I join in with this evaluation of "them," I am presupposing that I am content with my own lack of dogmatism or sense of my own rightness. What frees me to make a judgment about others and why they are unworthy of my mercy is the fact that I feel free from the thing I am condemning others for. If I am innocent, then I therefore feel empowered and emboldened to judge the guilty. This sense of self-righteousness—a powerful sense of moral superiority—is currently justifying many of the most merciless expressions of attacking perceived enemies of the Gospel or oppressors of the weak that I have ever witnessed.

Right now in our prayer lives, it is critical that we engage with Jesus' command to love our enemies. We are to pray for them, bless them with our words and serve them in meekness and humility. This is the most challenging element of the Gospel, but also the most beautiful. The plan of the Father is to establish a family filled with sons and daughters who love Him, and in so doing, who also display beautiful tenderness and mercy to others in an increasingly merciless world.

In all my years teaching about the Sermon on the Mount, loving our enemies is the command that folks most want to negotiate. Jesus put His very life into the hands of His enemies and emerged victorious in love. We are too afraid of what our enemies can do to us emotionally, financially or socially to love and serve them. I think we have arrived at a destination culturally where we feel that certain actions perpetuated by the "other side" exempt us from the biblical mandates to love. Ultimately, we need to wrestle with what Jesus meant by "love your enemies," and not find a justified escape because of what is done to us. If Corrie ten Boom could find the grace to love her tormentors and ultimately serve and bless them, why are we exempt when it comes to the possibilities of grace for loving our enemies?

Fear is not conquered by healthy boundaries. Fear is overcome by love perfected in us by God's grace. In renegotiating Jesus' terms for us to love others, we have removed mature love as our highest goal and have replaced it with self-care.

I want to emphasize here that I am by no means opposed to healthy boundaries, nor do I have an issue with us taking care of ourselves in a responsible manner. What I am opposed to is hiding behind terminology as a means of changing the terms of Jesus' command to love. We have made self-preservation a higher value than the command to take up our cross, and in the process we have used the sins of others to excuse our own sin. When we orient back toward self from a reorientation toward God, we will exaggerate our own sin in relationship to God's grace, but we will also exaggerate the sins of others in relationship to our own. We secretly and quietly do not feel justified by grace and the sacrificial love of God, who destroyed every boundary to secure our eternal destiny. It is therefore not uncommon for us to call attention to the sins of others in order to draw attention away from ourselves.

It is very important to acknowledge the difficult and delicate nature of discussions like these. There are some who interpret this kind of conversation as one that, like many others, contributes to perpetuating cycles of abuse and covering up sin, rather than breaking those cycles and exposing sin. The amount of suspicion, distrust and heartbreak involved in real situations where real, evil men and women have abused their power and authority is notable, and as a result this area is understandably difficult and tender to navigate.

It is also very important to note that when I talk about loving our enemies according to Jesus' command, I am not talking about abandoning civil and legal solutions that expose and end destructive abuses and wicked corruption. I am writing here about how we carry our hearts as the Church toward one another in our most wicked and broken moments. Civil authorities can and must intervene where and when legal boundaries have been violated. Law-breaking can and must be met with civil justice that reestablishes healthy societal boundaries, which in turn enable lawlessness to be restrained. Yet the ultimate and overarching cycles of abuse and control cannot be broken by worldly means alone. There must be additional solutions that express the beauty of God and His fierce, yet tender heart of perfect justice.

We so greatly need heavenly wisdom in the face of injustice, yet we are drawing more inspiration from one another than we are from the throne room of heaven as we look to both wield authority responsibly and address abuses tenderly but boldly. As I look around the Body of Christ, I see that we are stuck in cycles of sin and anger toward one another that address one issue only to replace it with another, with more being exposed than transformed. Cruelty in abusing power is met with cruelty in exposing it. Very few believers seem to be following Holy Spirit-led, biblical instruction and counsel in addressing sin.

How do we break out of this cycle and away from the flow of our culture, which is growing more loveless, merciless and cruel by the day? We need to grow in that wisdom from heaven, versus the confusion and "every evil thing" that are the products of what the apostle James called "earthly wisdom," which he identified as seductive but demonic (see James 3:13–18). I see earthly wisdom throughout the justice-oriented conversations and initiatives that are emerging in today's society to address racism, sexual abuse, misogyny and other sin issues beginning to come to light. People respond powerfully to this kind of wisdom because it seems to address the problems at hand in a way that reflects a moral and ethical stance, which produces actionable results within our current culture. Yet there is often an underlying layer of opportunism, envy, self-seeking, and ultimately confusion and evil as the ultimate response. In this case, I am calling evil any "justice solution" that does not produce a redemptive, restorative result. It is the justice of God if it works for anyone and everyone involved who is truly repentant. It is the justice of God if the solutions glorify and express the heart of the Father. Movements to expose abuse and oppression, and to expose and bring change to racial injustice, may have a sincere motive with just cause, yet still fail to bring forth a redemptive result. They will therefore suffer an evil ending.

We must look at even the most difficult, wicked and painful situations through a heavenly lens, rather than through a self-seeking one. This is the way to lay hold of wisdom from heaven, which God wants to pour out onto our lives and situations liberally. But we refuse that way because wisdom from heaven is often filled with truth that, in our pain and anger, we are not always prone to want to hear.

Wisdom from heaven, according to James, "is first pure, then peaceable, gentle, willing to yield, full of mercy and good fruits, without partiality and without hypocrisy. Now the fruit of righteousness is sown in peace by those who make peace" (James 3:17–18). This is the kind of wisdom with which God desires to fill His Church, which we express by loving others. According to Jesus in the Beatitudes of Matthew 5:9, peacemakers are reconcilers. They seek to repair relational breaches and help heal broken relationships. Our need to separate from a merciless culture is about more than refusing to entertain the merciless spirit of that culture; it is about coming into the fullness of expressing our love for others. God is jealous for that kind of expression of love and wants to put it on display through us for the earth to see.

There is a troubling problem, however, when it comes to acquiring true wisdom from above. A life filled with wisdom only comes from years of failure due to lack of wisdom. When I was younger, I read about the God of Israel's offer to young Solomon, son of King David and king of Israel after David's passing. The exchange between God and this new king in 1 Kings 3:5–14 is remarkable:

> At Gibeon the LORD appeared to Solomon in a dream by night; and God said, "Ask! What shall I give you?"
>
> And Solomon said: "You have shown great mercy to Your servant David my father, because he walked before You in truth, in righteousness, and in uprightness of heart with You; You have continued this great kindness for him, and You have given him a son to sit on his throne, as it is this day. Now, O LORD my God, You have made Your servant king instead of my father David, but I am a little child; I do not know how to go out or come in. And Your servant is in the midst of Your people whom You have chosen, a great people, too numerous to be numbered or counted. Therefore give to Your servant an understanding heart to judge Your people, that I may discern between good and evil. For who is able to judge this great people of Yours?"
>
> The speech pleased the Lord, that Solomon had asked this thing. Then God said to him: "Because you have asked this thing, and have not asked long life for yourself, nor have asked riches for yourself, nor have asked the life of your enemies, but have asked for yourself understanding to discern justice, behold, I have done according to your words; see, I have given you a wise and understanding heart, so that there has not been anyone like you before you, nor shall any like you arise after you. And I have also given you what you have not asked: both riches and honor, so that there shall not be anyone like you among

the kings all your days. So if you walk in My ways, to keep My statutes and My commandments, as your father David walked, then I will lengthen your days."

Simply put, when the Lord told Solomon to ask for his heart's desire, Solomon's heart desired wisdom.

What I assumed when I first read this passage is that the Father simply imparted wisdom mystically in fullness into King Solomon's being, and that suddenly Solomon was wise. Yet when I read about the rest of Solomon's life, and after this exchange Solomon's own words in Proverbs and Ecclesiastes, I was initially confused. These were not the actions and words of a man who was filled with heavenly wisdom for the entirety of his life as king. In fact, while his tenure as king of Israel had many successes, many profound failures happened under his leadership. These failures would ultimately impact Israel in very negative ways for many, many generations after his passing. His own son, Rehoboam, seemed to lack Solomon's wisdom completely, causing a catastrophic break between tribes that split Israel in two. Now I see Solomon's life and read his words differently. A "wise and understanding heart" (verse 12) spoke of his aptitudes. These enabled him to recover from his failures, be profoundly instructed by them and, with some pain and regret, pen some of the most powerful words of wisdom ever written. Ecclesiastes seems to reveal the futility of Solomon's foolishness and the perspective he gained on the meaning of life through living it foolishly. Proverbs reads now more like a book of tender regret, with Solomon seeking to pass on to his son the wisdom gained from the many mistakes he made as a king with a wandering eye for foreign women and the gods they worshiped.

When you read Solomon's works, you do not read the words of a man boasting of his many accomplishments. To read his words is to read the words of a man tempered and chastened by the failures that accompanied his many foolish choices. Yet the apex of his journey into profound wisdom culminated with the writing of the "Song of All Songs," or what the Holy Spirit inspired him to call "the Greatest Song Ever Written." (The title "Song of Songs" itself employs the ancient means of declaring that this is the greatest song ever written.) On the surface, it was a love song about a young bride and her royal bridegroom. For thousands of years afterward, rabbis, priests and later the early Church fathers, as well as the great theologians and scholars who would follow, understood the song as an allegory of the God of Israel's love for His weak, broken, yet sincere people who longed to love Him back.

The modern Church would have sought to silence, re-move or write Solomon off completely. Yet God found the mess of a sincere but foolish man's life and loved him faithfully to the end, producing the ultimate love song of God and His people. In the day-to-day of our journey to maturity in loving God, there is no way forward apart from time, patience and grace. The great heroes of the faith were afforded the time to grow and mature through fail-ure and the pain inflicted on them, and through the pain they inflicted on others in their brokenness. The Bible is honest about their brokenness. It is honest about the pain they caused. If one of the broken ones was our pastor or leader, it would be excruciating and frustrating to imagine giving them more time, more grace and more patience. The problem is that the ones leading in churches and ministries across the earth are the broken ones. Every single one.

There is a reason that the Father set His Spirit on Jesus and declared that He would be the one to bring justice to the earth (see Isaiah 42:1–4). A critical phrase in Isaiah 42 illustrates the primary reason that it must be Jesus and not any of us who brings forth justice. Isaiah prophesied, "A bruised reed He will not break, and smoking flax He will not quench; He will bring forth justice for truth. He will not fail nor be discouraged, till He has established justice in the earth; and the coastlands shall wait for His law" (verses 3–4). More than a few things are challenging about the way Jesus fights for justice and brings it forth. The delay is frustrating. *If He has all power and heavenly permission, why doesn't He act?* we wonder.

Even more frustrating—and this likely even angers us— is the way He brings justice to all with His heart of mercy for all. He therefore cares about mercy for the wicked, the oppressor, the abuser, the trafficker as much as He cares about deliverance and liberation for the oppressed, the abused and the trafficked. His slowness to act is connected to His mercy for all. If an oppressor, abuser, wicked man or wicked woman is a "bruised reed" who shows the possibility of being healed, or if the sinner is a "smoking flax" who has some hope of being restored into a fiery flame of love, then Jesus will move slowly related to justice, in hopes that the wicked will repent and be saved. Mercy and justice are united in His heart.

Yes, Jesus fights for the disadvantaged and the weak, but His heart is bigger and broader than ours in understanding who that is. His patient heart of mercy gives time for the foolish to become wise, the immature to grow into maturity, and the sinner to come to repentance and be transformed. We were once that person. We were undeserving of mercy, an oppressor and abuser in the making. Then we were loved with an extravagant love that we could never have earned, nor would ever deserve. We were forgiven. We were fought for.

We are loved as sinners who hated God. A life filled with the love of Jesus comes from years of fighting through pain, to continue choosing the risk of loving and serving weak, broken and therefore fundamentally unsafe people. We will continually fail the people around us, yet we will also recover and grow wiser because of it by the grace of God. The people around us will continually fail us, yet we can fight to "keep them in the game" through loyal love that reflects what Jesus showed us in our failures.

Our ultimate destination as a people is to display the transcendent love of Jesus to the lost through the expression of His kind of love to one another in the Church and through the Church. Jesus' agenda is to help us conquer our fears and deeply love a very unlovable Church. He accomplishes this by the impartation of His love into our hearts, helping us love the weak, the broken and the unsafe in the way that He does. This journey into transcendent love begins with and in Him.

Our Sympathetic Great High Priest

The writer of Hebrews stated, "We do not have a High Priest who cannot sympathize with our weaknesses, but was in all points tempted as we are, yet without sin" (Hebrews 4:15). Jesus experienced the pain of betrayal, the bitter wound inflicted by a trusted and dear friend. If we are to move forward and find real healing and power to overcome what has happened in our past, He must be our starting point and our object of long and loving meditation. He was wounded and afflicted, and He suffered, yet He overcame and was not overcome.

How did Jesus conquer the pain of betrayal and the wounding by a dear friend? How can we draw from Him and find healing and restoration, by His grace and power? Our comfort begins with the knowledge that because of His wounds, He sympathizes with ours. He is more than compassionate; He has experiential and personal history with what His friends have suffered at the hands of one another. He therefore suffers long with us in our weakness and in the way we wound others and injure our relationship with Him. He bears long with us, patiently and tenderly. What begins to change our lives and transform our perspective is the way that He sees both what was done to us and what we have done to others, as well as what we do to Him. He sees it all. Wounding was done to Him, and yet He did not sin. He did not dismiss or diminish the ones who wounded Him, nor did He withhold the fullness of His love and affection from them. As we wound one another, He bears with us in the same manner.

There is a powerful and haunting phrase in the gospel of John about Jesus' deep and overflowing love for those who would go on to wound and betray Him. The disciples have gathered into the Upper Room—likely the home of the young man who would eventually be known as John

Mark—and were about to have (though they did not know it) their last meal with Jesus before He would go to the cross. John writes, "Now before the Feast of the Passover, when Jesus knew that His hour had come that He should depart from this world to the Father, having loved His own who were in the world, He loved them to the end" (John 13:1) In the very next verse, John tells us that the devil had already put it into the heart of Judas to betray Jesus. Later, during the meal, Jesus makes it clear that He knows what is in Judas's heart to do and encourages him to go do it. Jesus knows that Peter is going to betray Him as well and tells him so. Jesus knows that filled with fear, unbelief and disillusionment, all His disciples will ultimately abandon Him.

Jesus knows what is about to unfold and knows fully what is in the heart of His friends. Yet on the eve of His painful death—a death in part orchestrated by the treacherous actions of a friend—He "loved His own who were in the world." He loved them "to the end." If you knew that your spouse was going to betray, abandon or abuse you, or that your leader or pastor was going to mistreat and silence you—if you *knew it fully in advance*—would you bring that person to an intimate meal, wash his or her feet and pastor that person through the pain of betraying, abandoning and losing you?

Jesus loved His friends in a way that challenges all our sensibilities and pushes the boundaries of what feels safe or wise. In the face of their coming betrayal, abandonment and pain, Jesus did not withdraw from His friends. He did not protect Himself from them or even confront them. He loved them, washed their feet and prayed for them. Yet most challenging of all, He opened His heart to them! This was the most intimate moment in Jesus' life up to that time. This was the most intimate meal that we know of. This was the most special conversation and the most powerful prayer time He ever shared with His friends. This expression of love from Jesus to those He cared so deeply for is beyond our comprehension or ability to reproduce and express to the people who might wound us.

Some might read this and be dismissive. "Sure, but this is Jesus," some might protest, arming themselves against His loving affections, lest they be forced into imitating Him. "He is different. He is perfect, and no one is perfect like that. I can't be like that."

What that statement really means is "I'm not supposed to be like that," or "I'm excused from being like that," because we are not special like Jesus or on a mission like His, nor are we fully God, as Jesus is. God is supposed to be this way. "Humans cannot—and are not supposed to—love this way," we maintain. "It's okay for God to love in such a risky, unsafe manner. He can take the pain of it all," we reason. This is the self-protecting, self-seeking logic of wounded ones eager to avoid being wounded again. We are desperate not to be fooled again into loving someone unworthy of love. Yet this is, of course, earthly wisdom.

The beauty of how Jesus loves His friends in this passage culminates with His prayer for them—and later, for all of us—in John 17. In that chapter, Jesus prays that the same love He possesses, the love the Father has for Him and the love He has for the Father, would also be in us. He prays that the way we love one another would reflect and express the way the Father and the Son have loved us. He prays, in other words, that the beauty that is in Him would be imparted to us, and that we would be made beautiful by His love and for the sake of love.

This kind of love is the ultimate end for the Church—washed by Jesus and transformed by His grace and beauty into a unified, open-hearted, tender and merciful people. A people who love meekness and walk in humility as they express His generosity to a hurtful, betraying, mercenary world of loveless, fearful, angry, self-seeking people.

It seems impossible. It is impossible. Yet Jesus' prayer in John 17 also tells us that it is probable, and that the greatest days for the Church are yet to come, in all her beauty, as a witness to this dying world. Jesus experienced the pain of betrayal, abandonment and horrible abuse at the hands of wicked leadership. He experienced the heartache of betrayal by His dearest friends. If you are hurting, angry and watching helplessly as your tormenter, abuser or betrayer seems to be getting away with it, with wickedness covered up and enabled by others, take heart. The God who became a man is not pitying you from a distance, waiting for you to get your act together. He is the sympathetic great High Priest who entered the human experience and suffered the worst of what humanity could inflict. The great warrior kings of old entered the fray and fought alongside their armies. Jesus, Son of David (the king who was the original warrior poet, as the sweet psalmist of Israel), entered the war against God that humanity has been waging for thousands of years. He entered the war on our side. He suffered and fought to love, in order to make a way for us to see our great hope and take heart.

Our great hope goes far beyond the hope of justice for those who wound or oppress or betray. As we see Jesus engage in our human experience as a man, we watch Him express the kind of power that is now available to humanity—to go far beyond forgiveness for those who wrong us, and touch the kind of outrageous, transcendent love that brings our hearts into a new and wholly victorious state of being. Jesus showed us that it is possible to be open-hearted, tender and gracious to betrayers, oppressors and abusers. He showed us what loving, blessing and praying for one's enemies looks like. By showing us these things, Jesus showed us what it means to be truly free. He showed us all what the Father originally intended it to mean to be human. Humans were never meant to be bound to those who sin against them, merely waiting and longing for a future day of vengeance to finally allow in their hearts the catharsis of satisfaction that justice would be finally and ultimately served.

Justice will finally and ultimately be served. That's true. It is a glorious truth. No one ever gets away with anything. The repentant acknowledge their sin and bow down to Jesus in surrender, asking for the justice of grace and transformation. The unrepentant refuse to turn or surrender, and they justify their wickedness and corruption, only to ultimately answer for it as they are confronted with perfect justice at the Judgment Seat of Christ. All those things are true and beautiful in what they express related to the perfect justice of God.

Long before those days, however, there is a glorious and hopeful day for the mistreated ones, the abused ones and the betrayed ones—today. Today is a day when we can experience the freedom of heart that human beings were born for. Washed by the blood of Jesus and transformed, our hearts experience the incomparable power of grace. This gives us the ability to begin loving in a way that goes far beyond "letting go." There is a power available to us that can take our hearts into the heights of beauty. Jesus loved His broken friends and bitter enemies as a man, to show us that it is not only possible, but that it is our destiny as a people bound to Him that we would love others the exact same way.

The Command to Love Our Enemies

In Matthew 5:43–48, Jesus sets what appears at first glance to be a high standard for His followers:

> You have heard that it was said, "You shall love your neighbor and hate your enemy." But I say to you, love your enemies, bless those who curse you, do good to those who hate you, and pray for those who spitefully use you and persecute you, that you may be sons of your Father in heaven; for He makes His sun rise on the evil and on the good, and sends rain on the just and on the unjust. For if you love those who love you, what reward have you? Do not even the tax collectors do the same? And if you greet your brethren only, what do you do more than others? Do not even the tax collectors do so? Therefore you shall be perfect, just as your Father in heaven is perfect.

Jesus seems to understand that this standard looks high, so He addresses the argument of the soul against His command. This is not, in fact, a high standard. While we feel victorious when we say nothing and refuse to retaliate or answer our enemies with evil in return, Jesus taught that the grace is available to us to go much further. We do not have to settle for a passive distance from our enemies.

The Pharisees removed "as yourself" from the commandment to love your neighbor (again, as one loves oneself), and in doing so they inserted the exhortation to hate your enemy. They were looking to establish a justification to love one another as Jews, while freely holding foreigners in contempt. They limited the command of Yahweh to loving people who were kind to them, treated them well and were like themselves (not to those who troubled them). They lived with revenge toward their fellow Jews and racism toward outsiders, instead of with God's all-embracing love.

In the Parable of the Good Samaritan, however, Jesus identified our neighbor as any and every human being, regardless of his or her race or religion (see Luke 10:29–37). Identifying our neighbor this way includes seeing our enemies as human beings and granting them all the dignity that goes with that designation. In our anger and bitterness, it is very easy to dehumanize our enemies and reduce them to their hurtful actions or ideas, versus seeing them in the light of all that they are to Jesus.

The call actively to love our enemies includes our words, actions and prayers. This is the highest summit of love and is much more than sentiment; it involves practical and continual actions. It is an act of our will, in partnership with God's grace that transcends our negative feelings. As we obey this command to love our enemies—with the help of the Holy Spirit by grace—our feelings will change. Loving people who hate us has the greatest impact at the deepest level—especially suffering for the sake of the Gospel, and ultimately, martyrdom.

Embracing this lifestyle opens the supernatural realm to us as we engage the available grace of God to transform our hearts to love the way He loves. Our enemies are adversaries who seek to hurt or hinder us, or who hope to see us fail. The apostle Paul wrote that "love suffers long and is kind," that it "is not provoked, thinks no evil," and that it "endures all things" (1 Corinthians 13:4–7). This is the kind of love God wants to impart into our hearts by the power of His Spirit as we yield to His will. This is the highest and most beautiful expression of love.

Jesus commanded us to bless those who curse us. We are to speak words of blessing to them and about them. We are to go beyond refusing to answer their insults with an insult. It can be a fierce struggle to speak words of blessing, but it will dynamically change and liberate us. We are commanded to do good to those who hate us, which means that we are to actively pursue practical ways to make their lives better. These commands kill our own fleshly instincts in pride and a lust for vengeance and offend our natural sensibilities. Our transformation on the inside really accelerates when we begin to pray genuinely for those who use us or persecute us. By praying for our enemies, we stand in the gap before God for them. This increases our love. It is impossible to pray for someone without loving that person, and then eventually connecting with the affections and perspective of Christ for him or her. Jesus prayed for His enemies as they were killing Him (see Luke 23:34).

We can overcome evil by doing good to our enemies, Romans 12:21 tells us. In verse 20, Paul quoted an Old Testament passage that commands us to love our enemies: "If your enemy is hungry, feed him; if he is thirsty, give him a drink" (see Proverbs 25:21). Jesus died for us while we were His enemies (see Romans 5:10). Our standard of love is to love as He loves, as we love our enemies without the condition of our self-interest. God loves people while they are unthankful and evil, instead of waiting until they are grateful. In loving this way, we become living proof to others that we have received the Father's love. We are filled with gratitude for His love that we did not deserve, so it makes sense to us to share that love with our enemies. This is the most convincing way to prove that the Father's love exists. It is God's grace to unbelievers to witness His love through you and me in the times when they mistreat us.

In praying for people who are in an adversarial relationship with us, we can encounter a resistance in our souls that forces us to go above the storm, to the big picture of truth. It is therefore critical to focus on key truths that can inject courage into our souls to stay with the Father's way forward rather than capitulating to the spirit of the age. We must entrust ourselves to God, knowing that Jesus calls us not to seek revenge when mistreated, but to endure it graciously.

How can we do this? We can endure graciously by trusting that God will vindicate us in His time and His way, as we commit the mistreatment to Him (see 1 Peter 2:23). No one has the authority to stop our God-ordained destiny. No Saul could stop David from his destiny; only David could stop David. We must fight and wrestle to see the bigger picture of our lives and the lives of our enemies. There is a bigger story unfolding than what our enemies have done to us. In fact, their lives and stories involve far more from heaven's perspective than the actions they have taken against us. Our greatest adversaries in the Body of Christ will be dear and cherished friends for billions of years in the age to come.

Unforgiveness, contempt and passive distance from our enemies all flow from the same perspective when we write them off. We see what they have done to us as who they are, and we see their actions toward us as defining the totality of their personhood. Also, we often declare in our hearts that what they have done to us is all they will ever be. We proverbially freeze them in amber, stuck in the moment that they wounded us or attacked us, and we leave them there until the end. Finally, we add to our perspective the declaration that, "This is who they are, this is who they will always be . . . *and the grace and love of God will never change that!*" We see their sin and sinful actions as more permanent than the grace of God, and we have no real desire to see them be transformed by His grace. We have little to no vision for our tormenters to be weeping and rejoicing at the beauty and glory of God and His great love. We view them this way because, to varying degrees, we view ourselves this way. We have little grace for ourselves in our weakness, and therefore we have no grace for others regarding their weakness—especially when it negatively impacts our lives.

Every person on earth has two narratives unfolding about himself or herself simultaneously. Every person you know has a "heavenly narrative," or the story God tells about him or her. Then there is the "demonic narrative," or the story the devil wants that person to believe about himself or herself. One of the great crossroads of your life has two significant elements to it: First, which narrative are you going to believe about yourself? Second, which narrative are you going to believe—and perpetuate—about others?

Are we going to fight to lay hold of the heavenly narrative and say about ourselves and others what God says about us? This reality lies at the core of intercession. We say back to God what He says about us and others, and what He wants to do in our lives to serve us into our destiny. There is, however, a demonic intercession that we can engage in regularly when we both agree with and perpetuate to others the wrong storyline about our enemies and those who trouble us. These enemies are more than what they are doing to us, and they are far more than what we think they are thinking about us.

One of the critical areas of victory and true freedom in our lives is the place where our enemies' sin has no hold on our hearts and no bearing on how we love. We can be exhilarated by the freedom to love our enemies. How? Simply by saying what Jesus says about them—by saying it to ourselves and others—and by seeing the bigger picture of who they are to Him and who they can be.

5

From Brokenness
to Beauty

The Song of Solomon, or "the Song of all Songs," is a
song about a young bride's journey into overcoming
her fears and pain and learning to trust the love and leadership of her new bridegroom. In the process, she comes
into a new place of maturity and capacity to love others
in a powerful and provocative way. Her love is provocative because of the way in which she is changed over the
course of the narrative from uncertain, insecure, fearful
and self-absorbed to selfless, confident, beautiful, faithful
and generous. These are just some among other changes
that she comes into as a beneficiary of her bridegroom's
love.

It is the way the bridegroom's love changes this bride
that causes her friends and those acquainted with her to

rethink the nature of her bridegroom and who he is. The onlookers, or observers of this bride's story, are forced to rethink both who she is in light of who she becomes, and who he is in light of her dramatic transformation, which is due almost entirely to his skillful love and leadership.

When the narrative structure of the Song is clear, it also becomes clear why it has been understood throughout history as a poetic depiction of Yahweh and Israel in rabbinic tradition, and of Christ and the Church in Christian tradition. In both traditions, it has been understood for centuries as a song about the love of God for His people, and what that love ultimately produces in the life of the Bride. This song is therefore a very helpful biblical construct in understanding where the Church is going from the Father's perspective. It is also a helpful lens by which to understand Old and New Testament prophetic declarations about the Church and the people of God at the time of Jesus' return.

In Church tradition, the first four chapters of the Song focus on the Bride of Christ understanding and enjoying her inheritance in Him. These chapters emphasize how God views and enjoys her. The last four chapters focus on Jesus' inheritance in the Bride. We seek something from Him, but He also seeks something from us. He wants us to love Him with all our heart. The focus of the book then completely shifts in the middle, when the Bride's prayer expresses profound dedication to Jesus and wholehearted trust in His leadership to bring her into her full destiny (see 4:16–5:1).

I have found over the years that the difficulty some have with this canonized, Holy Spirit love song is that they struggle to see its role and value in contributing to our ongoing spiritual vitality. The natural interpretation and descriptive language understandably become a stumbling block to receiving the spiritual and devotional benefits of the Song. Part of the key to appreciating this song's power and benefits are found in, again, remembering that it is canonized and therefore Holy Spirit inspired. As I said in chapter 4, the title that the Spirit inspired is "the Song of All Songs," or "the Greatest Song Ever Written."

What struck me about the power of the Song and its value to a believer's devotional life was seeing it as "the Old Testament book of Romans," and seeing the book of Romans as "the New Testament Song of Solomon." In other words, both books work together to describe how grace works in an individual (and in the Body of Christ). They also give a picture of what grace looks like over the course of our lives, as we decide to respond to God and His continued reach to love us and lead us passionately and jealously.

The "Old Testament book of Romans" speaks to the testimony of what the Gospel and the grace of God can produce in our lives. How far can the grace of God take us? How far can we go? The truths of the Gospel from the book of Romans are put to song here. They are applied to a young woman's story as she grows into mature love and obedience. Her story is our story, and in this song we can see the trajectory of grace and how high, how wide and how deep the love of Jesus can take us in our lives.

There are three themes that matter related to the grace of God and the power of the Holy Spirit: where I am going by grace, where are we going together and also where the

Church is going. The Lord is working with all His heart, soul, mind and strength to bring us into the fullness of His glory together as a family. He is very committed and passionate about the subject of the Church's destiny. He has a high vision for us as a family. We therefore want to ask, How far can the grace of God take the Church? How far in holiness and beauty can we go together?

The story of the young Shulamite girl and her journey of growing in grace and love gives us such a powerful picture of God's plans for us as believers in our lifetime, and for His Church at the end of the age. What does a mature Church look like before the Lord's return? How does it get there following His leadership?

The picture we see in this young bride's story is a picture of prayer and desire formed within the Bride of Christ's heart as she overcomes adversity, immaturity and compromise. Her song begins with her sincerity in serving others while neglecting to experience the love of Jesus herself. Every leader, servant and shepherd in the Body of Christ can relate to this.

The Bride's story also begins with failure that leaves her lacking in tenderness, compassion and grace for the very ones she is serving. She needs to be refreshed in the love and affection of Jesus, which is true of so many of us right now. The Bride experiences His love in a fresh and powerful way, after which Jesus calls her back into ministering and serving His people. She is afraid to respond because of her previous compromise and draws back. Yet she eventually repents and lays hold of a desire to obey at any cost, with a longing to give the fullness of her life and heart to Him.

Jesus responds to His Bride by proclaiming His deep love and affection for her in profound and specific ways. She is overwhelmed, and here she prays one of the most powerful prayers in all of Scripture. This propels the narrative or storyline of the second half of the book. We will examine that prayer in more detail in a moment.

Our first response when introduced to the Song is often one of perplexity. As we study the Song by faith, without enjoying it, initially its symbolic terminology can intimidate us. Over time, however, I believe it is possible to find much delight and pleasure in studying the Song. This happens as we encounter Jesus the Bridegroom and believe and feel the power of His love. This song has blessed the Church in this manner for many, many generations. The great Reformed preacher Dr. Martyn Lloyd-Jones stated this truth beautifully many decades ago in London:

> Has He ever said to you, whispered to you, "My Beloved is Mine?" Read the Song of Solomon and see how the Bridegroom expresses His feeling to His Bride, His love. How lightly we skip over these great statements so that we may argue about our pet ideas and theories! In one sense the whole object of being a Christian is that you may know the love of Jesus Christ, His personal love to you; that He may tell you in unmistakable language that He loves you, that He has given Himself for you, that He has loved you with "an everlasting love". He does this through the Holy Spirit. . . . What do we know of these secret intimations? Read the lives of the saints throughout the centuries and you will find that they all know about this. They have known Him to come to them and speak to them, and love them, and tell them that He loves them.

He embraces them and surrounds them, and lets them
know, more certainly than they know anything else, that
He loves them with all the intensity of His divine Being.
It is because we are married to Him that He does this.[1]

God's Amazing Plan for Our Small Lives

I heard many times when I was younger that "God loves
me and has an amazing plan for my life." In an American
context, this often meant some combination of a sense
of destiny, promotion, blessing and favor, and social and
ministerial success. I did not know back then as a new,
young believer that the Greco-Roman influence of Western
culture on the Church has created a highly individualized
sense of destiny for young believers. The modern reorientation from God as the center or heart of all things
to mankind as the center also contributes powerfully to
a sense of personal destiny, or "my destiny." As I began
to gain a better understanding of the Scriptures in their
ancient context, however, a very different story became
clear to me.

The Bible is meant to be understood as a collective story,
one shared by millions of very, very unique and different
individuals who often have nothing in common apart from
loving Jesus. When we have that shared reality, however, we
have everything in common that matters. The journey we
are on, into the highest and deepest places of pleasure and
joy in experiencing and maturing in the love of the Father,
is a journey that transcends history, culture, ethnicity or
financial status or station. Rich or poor, mighty or hidden, every man, woman and child around the world and

every person who has ever lived has a heavenly invitation to engage in this Gospel story of heart transformation.

When greatness in the eyes of the Lord truly is found in "first and great commandment" love and in Sermon on the Mount obedience, then anyone and everyone is a candidate to achieve this kind of greatness. Beyond the commonality of our collective journey, the corporate achievement of this end is the critical element of the Father's plan to vindicate His name amongst all who accuse Him, reject Him or diminish Him as the only Worthy One to rule the nations of the earth.

Our heavenly Father has an almost singular focus on His leadership of the Church. His consuming desire is to see all the saints walking in the fullness of Jesus' first and greatest commandment to love the Lord with all of their heart, soul, mind and strength. The Father's desire for us also happens to be the fullness of how we were made to function as human beings. The activity of the Spirit is therefore at work everywhere to stir and awaken love and a desire to please the Father everywhere that sincere love for Jesus can be found in this hour of history. Our common state in the present is that we are saved by grace through faith, filled with the Holy Spirit of God, and stirred by that same grace to love God with all our heart. Our common journey is to overcome the internal and external obstacles set before us in the world and to lay hold of mature love for Jesus, fully given to and obedient to Him, by His great help and leadership. While our occupation and ministry assignments can be a critical part of this journey, these areas are not the defining elements of our life in Christ. Our destiny is to be men and women who love Jesus. Our unique callings and destinies are far, far less critical in defining and shaping us in greatness than is this central calling to love, which is shared by every saint.

The apostle Paul understood this. As a Jew, his thinking prior to salvation involved a widespread, national salvation for all his people as they collectively expressed the Law of Moses together faithfully. Upon his salvation, this thinking did not shift to a Greco-Roman individualism. He would have seen intimacy with Jesus by Word and Spirit as the means for the collective Church to be joined together and empowered to accomplish this end. The Church would fulfill the Law by expressing the first and greatest commandment, the one that summed up all the commandments of the Lord and the whole of the Law. The Church's believers would come into the fullness of the love of Jesus, together.

This end informed Paul's prayer life and is therefore reflected in every one of his recorded prayers in his New Testament letters. Looking again at his prayer in his letter to the Ephesians, we can catch a helpful glimpse into his heart and, more importantly, into the heart of the Spirit in this present hour for the Church:

> For this reason I bow my knees to the Father of our Lord Jesus Christ, from whom the whole family in heaven and earth is named, that He would grant you, according to the riches of His glory, to be strengthened with might through His Spirit in the inner man, that Christ may dwell in your hearts through faith; that you, being rooted and grounded in love, may be able to comprehend with all the saints what is the width and length and depth and height—to know

the love of Christ which passes knowledge; that you may be filled with all the fullness of God.

Ephesians 3:14–19

This sets our individual journey into context. The key phrase in this prayer is that we "may be able to comprehend with all the saints" (verse 18). If we had a more pronounced sense of how truly connected we are in destiny, we would feel differently about the denominations and expressions of Christianity that frustrate us, or that we have written off entirely. The Baptists cannot come into the fullness of their destiny in Christ apart from the Assemblies of God. The Pentecostals cannot come into the fullness of their destiny apart from the Episcopalians. The fullness of God's plan for the Church cannot be fully realized without the whole Church. We must therefore wrestle through our temptation to exaggerate ourselves and our destiny, or worse, to dismiss ourselves and diminish our small but significant part in the plan of God for the Church.

We must grapple with what makes us valuable to God and what our place is in His family and in His plans for the immediate future. Our personal, intimate, individual journey into the grace of God unto mature love truly matters because each of us is very significant and valuable to God. Our prayer life matters. Our acts of service matter. Our fight to overcome offense—the pain of being forgotten, overlooked, misunderstood or mistreated—matters so much to the Father, who is championing our journey into being beautified by love. As we remember that God is moved, as we gain a clearer sense of why He is moved and as our longing awakens to go where He wants to take us, we grow in courage to stay with the long and arduous way into full joy.

When we understand the plan of God better, this way forward together makes much more sense. It is impossible to get the attention of the nations in a helpful way by powerfully transforming one man or woman, or even by igniting a handful of churches and ministries with the flame of holy love for Jesus. Bringing forth the fullness of the whole Church across the world in one generation, however, so that worldwide she would burn with deep, loyal, unshakable love for Jesus—this would shine forth as an irresistible witness to all peoples of the true beauty of Jesus.

When we understand the plan that all men and women who are in Christ share, we can find our place in a bigger story and take courage from a collective journey that we are all engaging in together. The courage I gain from this understanding empowers me to go on my individual journey into maturity in love for Jesus, because I can see where my weak, small journey matters in light of the Father's global plan.

God's Zeal to Conquer Our Hearts

This brings us back to the Song of Solomon. Many places in Scripture give expression and definition to where the Church is going in the fullness of her beauty and glory. Both the prophets of the Old Testament and the apostles of the New Testament had much to say about the journey of God's people out of sin, pride and compromise, into true devotion, purity of heart, humility and unfailing loyalty to the Lord. To restate what I presented earlier, what the Gospel and the Song of Solomon give us is a narrative progression that helps us understand where the grace of God can take us—both where we are going as individuals as we grow in love, and where we are all going together in the fullness of maturity enabled by grace.

The story of the Shulamite girl is a beautiful story of a bride propelled by the love of her bridegroom. In a broader context, it is also centered around the love of Jesus and the power of that love to bring us forth as His Bride into the fullness of joy and delight in Him and others. It is, surprisingly, also the story of how His Bride, His people, are washed by His love into truly—and deeply—loving the whole Church: leaders and elders, congregants, immature new believers and beyond.

As I stated earlier, this bride's story begins in both profound sincerity and profound weakness. She wants to love Jesus with her whole heart. Her declaration is one of dedication and devotion—her sincere intention is to pursue and follow Him all the days of her life. The young Shulamite bride fails almost immediately after this kind of declaration about her bridegroom. She becomes aware of her burnout and wrong priorities, caused by taking on too many responsibilities and fueled by the fear of man. This is true of the Bride of Christ as well, ultimately causing her to neglect her own interior life of love and devotion to Jesus.

This realization is likely one that the entire Church of the West needs to come to terms with, and it is one that any busy, overcommitted manager or leader can instantly relate to. The Bride knows that she has compromised, but she also knows two critical things: First, she knows that her Bridegroom enjoys her and calls her beautiful despite her weakness and compromise. Second, she knows that her way forward is with Him, rather than living at a distance from Him in shame.

The Bride makes a decision in the first chapter of the Song that is one of the key turning points in her journey with the Lord. She asks a critical question that changes her entire trajectory: "Why should I be as one who veils herself . . . ?" (Song of Solomon 1:7). In other words, she is asking, "Why should I be as one who lives at a distance from the One I love?" In asking this question, she expresses our part in partnering with the grace of God. Responding to the truth of who she is and why she is loved despite her failure, she believes. Therefore, she rises up and pursues.

This is a very important template for our own journey into mature love. We are not conditioned to handle failure well, in our prideful perfectionism and graceless, idealistic expectations of our spiritual vitality. The Bride demonstrates in this early part of the Song what true, radical faith looks like: believing that you are loved, cherished and valued by the King—and because you believe, you pursue, or you "fail" into the heart of Jesus rather than running from Him in shame. Faith is not merely something you demonstrate when you're waiting for things to turn around in your life. Faith is what you believe about Jesus and His love when you fail, and what you do about what you believe.

When the Bride encounters her Beloved, He shocks her—and us—with what He says about her related to her failure and compromise. He tells her where He can be found and invites her to join Him. He then tells her exactly what He thinks about her (and by implication, about us) in light of her failure. He tells her, in essence, that she is His favorite—the finest of the finest, the most excellent of saints.

This is not the answer the Bride was expecting after such a complete and utter failure to follow through on her commitments, and it is not the one that we expect when we fail, either. When we fail, we are certain that Jesus is quietly frustrated with us and dissatisfied with our interior instability. We can almost feel His impatience with us increasing with our every stumble and misstep. Here in the Song, He reaffirms the core of His identity and how He sees His Bride—as one who is far more as someone who loves Him than the sum of all her failures. Then He goes on to reveal why He feels this way about her.

What moves the Bridegroom about her love? On what grounds does He make such an audacious statement about who she is to Him? He extols the virtues of her emotions and choices—how she feels about Him and the many choices she has made to love Him—and He declares that these emotions and choices make her beautiful, like fine jewelry and gold. He declares that she has been one who has moved Him with her love, and He is specific about how and why, in her love, she is beautiful to Him.

This pattern continues throughout the early part of the Song. The Bride stumbles, and the Lord responds with extravagant love and specific details about why He loves her the way He does. She responds with more love for Him, overwhelmed by love so kind, gracious, merciful and extravagant. Her heart, slow to trust and filled with fear, is inexorably and deliberately delivered from that fear into profound trust. Her Lord's leadership accomplishes this remarkable transformation through His persistent, steadfast and transcendent love and affection.

As the story unfolds, and as we find ourselves in this story, a few key truths become very clear. First, this is the way Jesus wants to love us. He wants to wash us, relentlessly, with His extravagant love—even after we sin, stumble, fail or struggle.

Second, Jesus wants His love to produce something in us as it cleanses and transforms our understanding and emotions. He is fully, faithfully and unyieldingly committed to producing faith and confidence in us by stubbornly loving us into having a steady, fearless heart.

The progression of the Song's narrative does more than reorient our priorities and our definition of success and greatness; it reorients our understanding of how grace and the love of God work in our lives. As the apostle John wrote, "We love Him because He first loved us" (1 John 4:19). This order—love, leadership, sovereign initiative— matters greatly in understanding our life with God, how obedience and maturity are possible, and how we come into our full destiny in Him. If we don't understand that God desires to love us into a transformed heart and mind, we will labor to do our part without His help or initiative. Or worse, we will seek to perform His part in the relationship with all sincerity. So often, our Christian life is stunted because we try to obey God without a real relationship with Him, without an understanding of His Word, or without a revelation of His beauty that produces in us profound tenderness, responsiveness to His conviction and gratitude for His undeserved kindness.

We must wrestle in prayer with the truth of God's joyful, relentless pursuit of our hearts and His unyielding, faithful zeal in loving us on our best and worst days. He fights for us with joy and confidence in the potency of His love and skillful leadership, even when we ignore Him, forget Him, sin against Him or fixate on ourselves. He neither writes us off nor grows weary of the fight to fully capture our heart. Again, even more powerfully, He doesn't focus primarily on our deficiencies, our areas of weakness or the ways in which we fall short in loving Him back. He is filled with gladness as He defines our lives around the bigger picture of how our small, weak love moves His heart.

In Song of Solomon 4:9, the bridegroom exclaims, "You have ravished my heart, My sister, my spouse; you have ravished my heart with one look of your eyes." For the Shulamite, this revelation of the "ravished heart" of her bridegroom—overcome with love and delight because of one small glance from her eye toward him—is part of a longer series of profound encouragements he gives her that finally and ultimately conquer her heart. This is a picture of how the Lord wants to cleanse and conquer our hearts fully for Him. He overwhelms us with His extravagant love. He is more moved than we could ever imagine by our desire for Him, even if that desire from our perspective seems so negligible as to be nearly worthless. Thankfully, our Christianity and life with Jesus is not built on our perspective or our estimation of ourselves. Even more helpful is the knowledge that Jesus is not asking for our opinion in the formation of His own. He is our King, and His word about our lives, our love and how He values them is not subject to our vote. His word is the final word on the matter.

This is the Father's plan: to conquer the heart of every Christian who sincerely wants to know and love Jesus on earth and restore the first and great commandment to first place in the life of His Church. This is our shared destiny and our great calling as a people. We are going to be beautified together by the love of Jesus, and together we are going to express His beauty fully to an ugly, broken, hurting world filled with rage. This beauty, expressed in our love and His, is His greatest gift of mercy to a world that does not and cannot ever deserve it.

Divine Discipline, Surrendered Hearts

The turning point of the Shulamite bride's journey happens midway through the Song, at the end of the fourth chapter. She had been restored by the love of her bridegroom, yet at a key moment she chose her own path forward, trying to grow in love on her terms rather than submit to his wise and loving leadership. He lovingly disciplines her, withdrawing his presence from her.

To withdraw one's presence meant something very different in the ancient world than it would in, perhaps, a modern charismatic context. In the Old Testament, the Lord would "hide His face." "Do not hide Your face from me" is a common phrase used 34 times in the Law, the psalms and the prophetic books (see, for example, Psalm 27:9). Conversely, in the positive sense, a blessing was "let His face shine upon you and be gracious to you." "Shine the light of Your face" is a common blessing in the Old Testament, used over one hundred times throughout (see, for example, Numbers 6:25). This phrase was an indication of the Lord's favor, blessing and protection, whereas the hiding of His face, representing the withdrawal of His presence, was a removal of the favor that accompanied His intimate nearness to His people.

Why would the Lord withdraw His presence from His Bride in such a manner? Because God has no desire to endorse or enable the foolish or destructive choices we make in our pride and self-righteousness, which we feel are justified and wise in our own eyes. If the Lord were to continue to bless or show favor to us in such choices, or to deliver us prematurely from the consequences of our foolishness, it would cause us to grow emboldened in that foolishness.

The Lord therefore disciplines the ones He loves by— as the apostle Paul wrote in Romans 1—"giving us over" and "giving us up" to our own way (see verses 24–28). He allows us to engage in the foolishness of our own choices and wrestle with the consequences of our own actions. In this manner, as the apostle James wrote (as well as the apostle Peter), "God resists [opposes] the proud, but gives grace to the humble" (James 4:6; see also 1 Peter 5:5–6; Proverbs 16:5). Growing in humility is part of our journey that is as critical to the Father as our growing into mature love. Humility is the means by which we see ourselves rightly in comparison to others, versus making unhealthy comparisons borne of pride that exaggerates our deficiencies or our strengths.

This is how pride operates. It is the exaggeration of self, in the negative sense or the positive sense. It is also the distortion of self, which makes it difficult or impossible to have truly healthy relationships with others, especially with God. Humility is the means by which we relate to God in a healthy manner, as we properly and accurately understand our need for Him and His mercy toward us. The glory of humility that comes as a product of the Father's loving discipline is that we receive the necessary midcourse adjustments during our journey into beauty and mature love. This wholly converts us to trust in the Father's leadership in our lives, at the forsaking of our own way, including our stubborn opinions and wrong perspectives.

This is what happens to the Shulamite bride in the narrative of the Song, and in the bigger picture to the Bride of Christ. On the other side of her season of divine discipline, the Bride rises to pursue Jesus with hunger and humility, now convinced that His way is superior to her own. His loving discipline empowers her to overcome her fears, which had kept her in a prison of apathy and inaction. She braves the world and embraces risk to lay hold of the One she loves. When she finds Him, He finally and ultimately conquers her heart with an explosion of joyful encouragement and specific observations about who she is and how her love moves Him.

This brings us again to the end of the Song's fourth chapter, where the Bride has overcome compromise and fear by the excellence of the Bridegroom's leadership and the irresistible power of His transcendent love. She wants to be fully given in love, which means that she wants to be fully His, for Him to spend as He will on others in ministry and mission. Therefore, she prays one of the most beautiful prayers in Scripture, inviting the winds of divine activity—warm, refreshing winds of blessing, as well as the colder "north wind" of difficulty and testing—to move powerfully on the garden of her heart (Song of Solomon 4:16).

The Bride started with mistrust, reserved because of her fear and independent of her Bridegroom's leadership. But now she has gone to being fully open, and being confident that whatever happens next, according to His sovereign wisdom, she will be empowered to love Him with all her heart, soul, mind and strength. She is now fully surrendered to this cause, and fully trusting that His leadership will take her into those heights and depths. She cannot take herself there; she cannot produce that kind of love from within herself. She herself is incapable of the kind of spiritual performance that could escort her into the depths of where only God can take her. She therefore says, with genuine authenticity from spirit and truth, *Anything that You want to do to produce greater love in my heart for You—I say yes!*

This is where God is bringing you (and me). With all His love and tenderness, with joy and no rejection in His heart for you, His earnest desire, with all holy jealousy, is to bring you to the place of true and complete surrender to His leadership. He wants to cleanse you of all pride that exalts your own opinion, and from all driven perfectionism that steals all joy from your pursuit of Himself. He wants to escort you to the place of deepest satisfaction in Him, and to the heights of complete and utter delight and joy in His beauty. He wants to remove every hindrance in your understanding, emotions, brokenness, immaturity and beyond.

This happens to the measure that you and I open our hearts to Him and engage with His grace, versus living the daily life we so often live as functional agnostics— Christians who are saved by grace and who love Jesus, but who live continually separated from the life of His Spirit and the fire of His Word's truth. By praying the prayer that the Bride prays, *Let my Beloved come to His garden*, we invite the presence and activity of the Spirit into our lives in a greater dimension (see Song of Songs 4:16). The Bride is not content with the hidden, imperceptible ways that God loves her and helps her daily. She wants a conscious, active awareness of and connection to His loving help and sovereign leadership. She wants to perceive Him more and open her heart and life fully to invite Him to do more. She wants deeper joy and the gift of tears. Why tears? Tears are an indication of a tender heart. We shed them when we are moved with deep gratitude, or when we experience mourning and loss. Tears are the indication of an alive, connected heart. We want the kind of joy that moves us to tears, and the kind of heart that is moved to tears easily. We need the Holy Spirit to escort us to the place where we are deeply and profoundly moved by God and His love. Rather than trying to go somewhere in God, the Bride is now chastened and wiser, asking Him with her whole heart to take her to such a place.

The Bride's love, always beautiful to Him, has reached a place of true beauty that will now be evident to all who know her. Her love, small and weak such as it was, has grown. She has grown. In seeing the Shulamite bride's progression, we can see clearly where grace and the love of God can take us as the Church as well. You and I can be filled with hope again that a glorious future awaits us that lies far beyond our present and future circumstances. The great unanswered question, however, in the young bride's life and in ours, is the question of how we know that there has been progress. Our lives, our hearts and our love are being made beautiful by grace and the power of the Holy Spirit, but the transformational progress is mostly internal and not evident to the eye. Have we been transformed? While our love may be more pronounced, we still feel like "us" when we wake up in the morning and engage in our day. We still feel as if we are on a journey with "ourselves," and we do not feel all that different when considering our weakness, brokenness and deficiencies.

Yet in this greatest of songs, the Bride is on the cusp of a catalytic moment in her life that will propel her in an accelerated way into her full destiny. She has been transformed, but she does not quite know it. She has become beautiful by grace, but she cannot quite see it. Those around her are in the same predicament. Their friend has been radically transformed by grace and love, but they are—like everyone else we know—too self-absorbed to see what God has done. Therefore Jesus, in His perfect, brilliant leadership, is going to allow a scenario to unfold that answers His Bride's prayer—*send the north winds . . !* This will reveal His handiwork in us.

This is going to bring about the most difficult season of the Bride's life, but the trial will be worth it. She has already gone from weak, immature love to the provocative love of a conquered heart. Now, with great delight and satisfaction, Jesus is going to show the world exactly what He has done.

6

"There, I Will Give You My Love"

Several years ago, I entered the darkest and most difficult season of my life. It was one of those seasons where nothing seemed to be working, from our personal finances, to frustrating workplace dynamics, to culminating in a series of catastrophic and painful events that were far, far beyond my control to help or to stop.

Up to that point, I had experienced many seasons where my immaturity, inexperience and profound lack of wisdom stirred up complex relational dynamics and collisions that made my need for growth and maturity quite evident. I had known, in other words, what it meant to suffer and bear long with the consequences of my own lack of wisdom and naiveté. This season of my life was much different. Events outside my control, combined with the consequences of other people's actions, stirred up much controversy and trouble in my life. Controversy, accusation, pain and relational tensions with dear friends erupted around me and made life hellish and awkward at every turn.

Many days during that season, I did not want to get out of bed.

The ministry that I loved and loved engaging with was suddenly stripped of all its joy for me. Long, difficult meetings and hard conversations and confrontations took every ounce of my energy. It seemed as if I was in the fight of my life, but I didn't know how to win and I didn't know when it would end.

I vividly remember the feeling I had one morning—the distinct and painful realization that I did not have the strength to endure the trouble one more minute, yet there was no sense that things were going to change for many, many years to come. It was an awful moment. I broke. The way I have explained that season to friends over the years is that I had grown used to "paying the bill" for my own stupidity; however, this was the first time that I was "paying the bill" for trouble I had not caused. As I labored to serve in that season, working to "pay the bill," I felt utterly bankrupt and empty.

The Darkest Night and Grace of God

I did not know it at the time, but that season was a very, very small-scale and personal version of what Saint John of the Cross, a sixteenth-century Catholic mystic, called "the dark night of the soul." That phrase has come to mean various things to various commentators and observers over the years, who have mostly reduced the concept to a personal, existential crisis. There was an element of that in Saint John's poetry and writings. What he had in mind, however, was more about the kind of existential crisis God Himself causes or allows as part of a season of divine testing. This kind of season of "testing our love" was, in Saint John's view, very different from a season of divine discipline. This was primarily because of the way such testing is designed to help us on our journey toward beauty and maturity, which he understood as a "mystical union" with God.

This kind of testing season—which, again, is what the Bride prayed and asked the Lord to send into her life at the turning point of the Song of Solomon—does not involve tests that God gives us to teach us something, humble us or cause us to fail. Those elements of our growth are the kinds of things God works on lovingly during seasons of divine discipline. Seasons of testing such as John of the Cross wrote about, however, serve a different purpose. They are primarily about revealing that which is hidden, so that God's handiwork might be clearly seen, for the encouragement of many.

"Testing to reveal that which is hidden" does not sound exciting to most of us. We tend to live with quiet gratitude over how much of what we know about ourselves is generally unknown to those around us. Thankfully, true love "will cover a multitude of sins" (1 Peter 4:8; see also Proverbs 10:12; 17:9). Jesus is not out to embarrass us. He is not wanting merely to expose us and humiliate us into seeing things His way. He is the gentle and tender Good Shepherd, skillfully navigating the complexities of our weak and broken hearts to bring forth the highest and deepest expressions of fiery love possible. His desire is our repentance and transformation.

Therefore, the season of testing that John of the Cross—and prior to him, King Solomon—wrote about involves both the refining of our motives for pursuing Jesus, and the revealing of His glorious work in us, to us and to those around us.

The apostle Paul wrote about this in his letter to the Romans:

> Therefore, having been justified by faith, we have peace with God through our Lord Jesus Christ, through whom also we have access by faith into this grace in which we stand, and rejoice in hope of the glory of God. And not only that, but we also glory in tribulations, knowing that tribulation produces perseverance; and perseverance, character; and character, hope. Now hope does not disappoint, because the love of God has been poured out in our hearts by the Holy Spirit who was given to us.
>
> Romans 5:1–5

He wrote similarly to the Corinthians:

> Blessed be the God and Father of our Lord Jesus Christ, the Father of mercies and God of all comfort, who comforts us in all our tribulation, that we may be able to comfort those who are in any trouble, with the comfort with which we ourselves are comforted by God. For as the sufferings of Christ abound in us, so our consolation also abounds through Christ.
>
> 2 Corinthians 1:3–5

What Paul was pointing us toward is the invitation to know deeply and intimately the "Father of mercies and God of all comfort" during suffering and trials. We need to grow in our intimate, experiential knowledge of the Father, the source and giver of mercies and the God of all comfort—comfort being more than something that He offers us. Rather, it is built into the core of who He is. He is full of comfort and strength, and He longs to establish us in it even before crisis and storms afflict our lives.

Likewise, we are called to be vessels of comfort and consolation to others in their storms in the coming days. Yet we will only give comfort according to where we ourselves are comforted. This is the reason we become evangelists for the books, resources or people who have inspired or helped us when we faced great pain and trial in our lives. We found comfort in their example, their principles or their experiences, which gave us courage to endure rather than quit. In turn, we comfort those around us with those same resources.

How can we find comfort and consolation during crisis, difficulty and pain? We must fight to lay hold of true comfort, finding rest and help from the Lord today so that we might be useful to the people we care about during their trials tomorrow. Comfort during trials and difficulty is more than freedom from anxiety, fear or negative emotions so that we can lay hold of a sense of peace. The consolation that abounds through Christ is a powerful anchor of truth and confidence that we can walk in. It connects us to the zeal and intensity by which He fights for us and causes all things to work for us, for our good and for our destiny in Him.

Our present affliction and current pressures can work for us and strengthen our glorious hope, rather than diminish our hope or serve as a negative confession. We often define our future according to our perception of our current circumstances. Paul wants us to know that our new life in Christ is our escort into a great future apart from—and no longer defined by—our present circumstances. Our lives are now defined by the commitment of God to bring us into our great destiny and future fullness in Him.

In other words, our right behavior is not the starting point or the initiator of the activity of the Spirit and the power of God in our lives. Our right behavior is the *fruit* of our confidence in His love and our response of cooperating with His grace. We become "settled" and confident in love, despite negative circumstances, when we continue actively connecting to who God is and what He has done.

In other words, as saints we must understand that the suffering, trials and tribulations the world around us inflicts on us—and the available grace from God to go far beyond enduring trials to being transformed by them—are necessary in order to impart the fullness of God's beauty into our lives. Because our confidence is according to the Gospel, and because we have a different perspective about our future, when trials come, we can rest and allow grace to put negative circumstances to work in our favor. We can allow tribulation and trouble to produce something in us that we will be thankful to God for, forever.

We do not tend to think of tribulation and trouble as an occasion for God to do something in us or reveal something about us. We just want the difficulty to stop and are committed to complain until it does. Gratitude and hope are often the farthest thing from our minds. This is where I found myself in my season of testing, trial and difficulty. I wasn't primarily focused on thanking God for the season I was in; I just wanted it to end.

Yet through the different waves of difficulty and controversy I faced, I was surprised by two things. First, I was surprised by the available grace for my interior transformation in the areas Paul spoke of in Romans 5. I noted the grace I was given over time for perseverance, to bear long and bear with, even when things felt unbearable. I noted the grace I was given on the inside for my character to shift, as I became far less defensive and far more willing to be a blessing to my accusers and to engage them with a genuine desire for their good. My perspective began to change, and hope became real to me. Even now, years later, the Lord is still surprising me with twists and turns to the story that leave me filled with genuine hope for the most redemptive outcome to some very difficult situations and stories.

Moreover, I found my motives for serving and ministering to others being refined as blind spots and areas of weakness, and immaturity came to the surface under pressure. Although I didn't cause the trouble and conflict I found myself navigating, looking back, I can clearly see the benefits of the crisis from the Lord's perspective. It is one thing to pray, *Lord, I am in this for love as my highest end*, and sincerely mean it to a degree. A season of intense trial and testing, however, can amplify and clarify other unperceived or unhelpful reasons that we serve and minister. In persevering, I was signing up for more than

119

bearing long and not quitting; I was "re-signing up" for the original reasons I had begun pursuing the Lord in the first place, during the days of my early encounters with His love and grace. In key moments, gratitude touched my heart for Him, for His kindness and even for His love and affection toward those who were bringing affliction into my life.

This brings me to the second thing that surprised me during my season of trial and controversy: the testimony of my closest friends, whether they were observing what was happening to me from up close or from some distance. Add to this the testimony of acquaintances, observers and folks who would encourage me seemingly out of the blue. Whether folks knew what I was going through or not, I was moved by the number of times the Lord would stir them to bring an observation about positive changes they had seen in my character, my heart and my love for others.

Prior to my season of testing and trial, I had little to no "eye" for the beauty of God's work within me. I was either too self-absorbed over my perceived deficiencies, or I was too frustrated with my unresolved areas of unfulfillment and my desire for change. Or else I was too focused on areas of deficiency in other people who were making my life complicated or difficult. I couldn't appreciate what God had done and was doing in my life to draw me into beauty. I therefore engaged the day-to-day of marriage, work and friendships without the necessary tenderizing agent of gratitude, the calming agent of perspective or the bigger picture of God's fiercely tender heart of love for the weak and the broken, whom I mostly viewed as the source of many problems.

I fell into the same trap that I see many stumbling into right now. I had unlimited compassion for the people being hurt, but no compassion for the leaders, pastors, employers or any of those in authority who had a very, very difficult task to accomplish. I could tell the story of how certain leaders had mishandled people, but the Lord eventually had to help me also tell the story of the behind-the-scenes dynamics of why they had done it. He also had to help me tell their story to my own soul with His tenderness and mercy.

The pressure I was under revealed that a good bit of my self-perception was very wrong, very limited or very focused on the wrong things. Other things were true about me that I couldn't see, but I assumed that God would think the best of me in areas where I had been blindsided by others. Eventually, even a few of my enemies began to see the best in me, or see areas of transformation in my life that I was barely aware of myself. For some people, it was like seeing me after a sudden, dramatic weight loss. Their exclamation of surprise at my newfound tenderness of heart held a sting of realization for me as I realized how they must have viewed me before. Over time, however, my close friends also confirmed on their own what others were saying about me. During my trial, somehow, by the grace of God, a transformed way of loving others—a way markedly different from my younger years—was shining forth clearly to them.

The Mature Love of a Tested Bride

Now let's return to our Shulamite bride and the Bride she foreshadowed. When we saw her last, the Bride had come to a powerful moment of true surrender in her life, not just yielding to her Lord's leadership out of duty, but out of a powerful revelation of the superiority of His safe leadership and incomparable love and commitment. As Paul wrote in Romans 5:1–5, she saw her life as one fastened to His, and now she understood that her destiny and future was truly in His skillful and wise hands.

The Bride had also come to realize that the areas where she did not trust her Lord's leadership happened to be areas where she subconsciously assumed that she was wiser than He. No longer. She now knows the truth: His love is the safest place to be, and her future as one who fully loves Him can only be realized by His leadership. Like the Bride, we must come to the realization that, while we might argue and negotiate terms with God's commands for a while, eventually we will yield voluntarily to His far superior wisdom and the way in which He brings us into mature love.

When I look back at the worst season of my life—one that I would never want to see repeated in any way—I still look at God's handiwork in my heart and perspective during that season. When I look at what He produced in me and others, I marvel and thank Him. I am a sound convert to the brilliance of His ways and the righteousness of His commands. While my flesh still resists some of those commands, I cannot argue against the fruit of pleasure, beauty and joy that they have produced in my marriage, family, friendships and working relationships. The tenderness of the Lord to bring me into His beauty, and the reflection of that beauty in my relationships, is worth far, far more than premature relief from yesterday's pain. I am thankful that His leadership ran its course in my life, and that He is still diligently, patiently and joyfully at work within me to continue His beautifying work in me.

Returning to the Shulamite, we see that her story (and therefore ours as the Church) accelerates significantly during the second half of Solomon's song. She endures her own season of severe testing, being mistreated by leaders who misunderstood and misinterpreted her pursuit of her bridegroom. They are misguided and heavy handed. Her friends are horrified and are ready to join her cause and be a sounding board of complaint and counterattack. Yet something remarkable happens next. She is so filled with longing and a deep ache for more of the love of her bridegroom that she does not engage their observations about what happened to her at all. She seems to have no mind for it; her response to her friends seems to indicate that she is almost unaware of what was done to her. Her friends seem to realize in this moment that the leaders who struck her were not the only ones they had an issue with. They had an issue with her Beloved. They are confused by the Shulamite and her deep affections and longing for the one who seems to have abandoned her without cause.

The Shulamite's response is one of the high points in all of Scripture. Song of Solomon 5:10–16 is the moment in which she bursts forth with a powerfully detailed picture of her bridegroom's beauty—which echoes for us the Bride of Christ's declaration of the beauty of Jesus. It is clear from the Bride's depth of intimate knowledge and understanding of Him that, while her friends may know *of* Jesus, she profoundly knows Him. Her intimate knowledge of her Bridegroom comes spilling out of her heart, with incredible detail and stunning beauty. She is not simply reciting facts or memorized verses, or repeating a sermon about Jesus that she once heard. Her experiential, intimate knowledge of Him is both alive within her heart and able to be communicated beautifully under pressure. She describes Jesus powerfully to her friends as the incomparable, matchless, singular Bridegroom.

In 1668, the great Scottish preacher James Durham described the Bride's words in this manner:

> Whence, Observe, 1. That Christ is the most lovely and excellent object that men can set their eyes on, that they can cast their love and affection upon: there is not such a one as Christ, either for the spiritual soul-ravishing beauty that is in him, or the excellent desirable effects that flow from him. O what a singular description is it which follows, if it were understood! 2. Christ is the most singularly excellent Husband that ever was closed with: under that relation he is commended here, as singularly lovely, and loving; it is a most honourable, comfortable, happy, and every way satisfying match to have him for a Husband. 3. Christ's worth in itself is not expressible, and whatever he can be compared with, he doth exceedingly surpass it.[1]

Finally, the great Puritan preacher George Burrowes compared this passage of Scripture to the finest sculptures ever carved or the most beautiful paintings ever set to canvas. The words of Solomon represent the very heights of beauty itself, personified in Christ:

> Wishing to set forth to mortal eyes the beauty seen in Christ, the wisdom of God, the Holy Spirit represents

these not in marble that may be mutilated, and may perish, but in language that can never die; and gathers in this language the most beautiful comparisons and richest expressions possible. Could no other reason be given for inserting these passages in the Scriptures, this would be sufficient—that Christians of undoubted piety, deep experience, and great purity of heart, have found these illustrations of the loveliness of Christ, a source of instruction and unspeakable delight—not only not suggesting unhallowed thoughts, but feeding the soul with meditations kindred with those of heaven.[2]

The Bride has been mistreated by her leaders, yet she is very clear in her deeply moving and detailed praise of Jesus that she knows what is really going on. His safe leadership has allowed a context for her to step into a newfound confidence and maturity, a beauty and transformation that displays the splendor of what He has done in her and why she so deeply loves Him. She is on display for all of her friends and leaders to see. What they see is the handiwork of Christ's excellence, the riches of His grace and His incomparable love. She knows Jesus in a profound, provoking manner that effortlessly challenges the depths of their own relationship with Him. Their only rational response is a hunger and longing for the same, provoked in their pursuit by the evidence of grace in their formerly immature, weak and broken friend, the Bride. Her dramatically different radiance and beauty is proof of the superiority of the Gospel and the love of Jesus, and is the evidence of our profound need for Him to work the same way within us.

What follows is yet another controversy, as some in the Church are at odds over the Shulamite's beauty and authenticity. Two camps form around her reputation, as the narrative of the song reads, with each camp representing opposing views about her trustworthiness and authenticity (see Song of Solomon 6:13). She does not answer the cry that has erupted about her life, and in the next section her Lord answers and vindicates her as one who has loved him fully and beautifully.

What happens next is as remarkable as the Shulamite's earlier response to testing, and in it, as we have seen throughout, she mirrors the Bride of Christ. Rather than pausing to enjoy the love of the Bridegroom expressed powerfully over her life at the beginning of chapter 7, the Bride is stirred to take hold of Jesus and bring Him to others within the Body of Christ, those who used and misused her in the first chapter. These are the ones who misunderstood and mistreated her a few passages earlier in the song—the same ones who, in the previous paragraphs, still erupted in meaningless and fruitless controversy around her and her ministry.

Yet her heart is fully conquered, and her life is fully His:

> I am my beloved's,
> And his desire is toward me.
>
> Come, my beloved,
> Let us go forth to the field;
> Let us lodge in the villages.
> Let us get up early to the vineyards;
> Let us see if the vine has budded,
> Whether the grape blossoms are open,

And the pomegranates are in bloom.
There I will give you my love.
Song of Solomon 7:10–12

The evidence of a heart fully conquered and completely given in surrendered love to Jesus is a heart that is eager and energized by tenderness and affection for His Church, to get up early to serve the Church. Very few verses in the Bible move me like Song of Solomon 7:12. After all that the Bride has gone through, she sees the members of her Body in all our brokenness, all our immaturity, a profoundly unsafe place to be at times because of what cruel people are capable of . . . and she is energized with desire to love Jesus *there*. In the midst of her people. Unafraid.

John the Beloved wrote about this in 1 John 4:17–19:

Love has been perfected among us in this: that we may have boldness in the day of judgment; because as He is, so are we in this world. There is no fear in love; but perfect love casts out fear, because fear involves torment. But he who fears has not been made perfect in love. We love Him because He first loved us.

Mature or perfected love looks like fearlessness. The enemy of love is not hate, though many in our day are using that idea as a means of controlling others. Hate is one of the worst things a person can express in our day, and entire marketing campaigns are working night and day to eradicate hatred. Yet because of love, God hates the enemies of love in our life. He hates everything that stands between Him and us as His dearest friends, anything that might get in the way of our glorious eternal future together.

The God who hates anything that opposes His love is fearless and not indifferent or passive in the patient but fierce removal of all His enemies who refuse to repent or move aside. Fear is the great enemy of love. Fear of what might happen if we risk loving others. Fear of what they might do to us or take from us. Fear of being exposed. Fear of losing friends and influence. Fear makes us indifferent, uncaring and passive in the face of evil. The picture of the love of the mature Bride in Song of Solomon 7, one whose heart has been fully conquered by the love of Jesus, is a picture of fearlessness. She is not fearless regarding believing in her dreams. She is not fearless regarding believing in herself. She is fearless when faced with everything Jesus is passionate about and gave His life for. Having come to the other side of profound growth and testing, she has decided that she wants to lay her life down as well.

Beauty is not reflected in the face of the fierce self-love and unapologetic "be yourself" charges that fill our culture. Beauty is defined by a life fully and utterly transformed by the love and leadership of Jesus, a life now willing to lay itself down for a friend—and an enemy. There is no greater love than this.

The challenge and invitation we are faced with is the call to go the same way, embracing our own cross for the sake of love. While it is encouraging to find my story in the story of the Shulamite, mine are only very small reflections on a much bigger story, the story of the Church. Every Christian you know personally is on some stage of this journey as well, whether he or she realizes it or not.

When we are resolved that loving Jesus and His Church fearlessly is the only rational way to live our lives in such an hour as this, our hearts begin to shift. We must be resolved in our understanding that the One whom we love is unyieldingly committed to bringing every Christian on earth on this same journey. In other words, we can become so consumed with our own journey that others around us are reduced to those who merely help us or hinder us as we progress. We must instead lay hold of the fierce, jealous love of Jesus for those around us—even in their weakness and brokenness. As we do, the result will cause us to think of our lives and other believers' lives very differently.

My great hope is that one of the culminating attributes of the Bride at the end of this particular story—a deep, unshakable love for the whole Church—so fills the earth in the coming days that all peoples must stop and reckon with the true nature of the God-Man from Nazareth. I am confident that it will. When it does, I want to be at the heart of it all, and I want to be right there with you.

PART TWO

BEAUTY OVERCOMES DARKNESS

7

The Rejection of God's Beauty

Up to now, we have explored the individual and corporate journey of the Church as we progress together into mature love and a transformed life infused with God's beauty. From here, it would be helpful to shift to the future of the Church and the stunning conclusion of God's plan for the global Body of Christ, and, by extension, for you, me and our children in the days to come. The more clarity I gain from the Word and the help of His grace, the more in awe I am of God and His mercy and skillful leadership.

The core idea of this book is that God is going to take the beauty that He possesses and impart it into His Church, so that the earth has a very clear and inarguable picture of who He really is, how He really loves and the kind of world He wants to build with His people. Think of God's labors to purify and nurture His people as a means of pleading His case with the nations of the earth (see Jeremiah 25:31). God gave the world His Son as an expression of His great love, that "the author and finisher of our faith" would in turn establish the means via the cross for the indwelling Spirit to work in God's people, that they might also be fully given as His gift to the world (Hebrews 12:2).

It seems impossible to believe that the Father could produce a Church that loves like His Son Jesus, before Jesus returns to the earth. The great tragedy of a broken and sinful world is that they will do to the Church what they did to the Son of God. The great miracle is that the Church will respond to this wicked rejection and brutal persecution—a true, global "dark night of the soul" moment for the Church—with unprecedented love, mercy, forgiveness and tenderness toward her enemies. God will declare through His people the full measure of what His grace, love and beauty can produce in the human heart. It will be the ultimate apologetic for who God really is, one that we will remember and be deeply grateful for and profoundly moved by for all eternity.

How could the Father establish such an expression of beauty in His people—one never seen before, to this magnitude, in the whole of human history—only for wicked men to trample the garden He produces underfoot? How could humanity despise both the magnificent offer of the free gift of righteousness through the cross and blood of Jesus, and spurn that offer personified beautifully by the Church at the end of the age? Why would people willingly choose ugliness and spurn beauty?

The good news—the very good news—is that not everyone will despise the beauty of the Lord displayed through His Church. Many will see it, fear the Lord, repent and be saved. Then they will be able to enter into that beauty now and forever. Out of all the ways to appeal to humanity, this plan of God to display His beauty through His people is the most effective means of touching the coldest, darkest of hearts. Yet for many, the beauty of God will provoke them to run even harder in the direction of their own agenda. What is the future of the Church in light of this growing darkness? She needs to continue her journey into her Bridegroom's beauty, drawing those who are lost in the ever-increasing darkness of this present world toward the light of His incomparable love.

The Descent into Greater Darkness

The journey of the Bride into love and beauty in the Song of Solomon, culminating with a wholehearted commitment to love the other members of a very weak and broken Church with the same love that Christ possesses for her, was also understood by the priestly authors of much of the Old Testament as an ascent. One would "go up" to, or ascend, the mountain of the Lord, entering into His ancient house—"the dwelling place of the Lord." This pictured the way of Moses and the ascent of humankind into the heights of holiness. National obedience to the Law of Moses, with loving care and detailed devotion, was understood as the fullness of one's national duty. The ache of the ancient Hebrew's heart was for God to dwell fully on the earth again, as He did in the Garden of Eden at the beginning.

The first chapter of Romans summarizes the opposite journey—the movement of the human heart away from God. Paul presents this journey away from God as a descent, one in which the Father gives people up and over to their base desires, foolishness and rebellion. God does this in hopes that they will come to their senses, turn from their wicked ways and embrace the wisdom of His boundaries, laws and leadership. If the Church has been on a long journey toward beauty, the knowledge of God and the riches of His love and grace, the world has been on its own ancient journey. From the Garden of Eden, the great tragedy and controversy of humankind has involved our collective desire to build a world and a society without the presence or person of God. Our accusation against His character and nature, which we'll look at more closely in a few moments, bolsters and justifies that corrupt desire.

Paul is explicit and clear in defining immorality to illustrate humankind's descent into rebellion and wickedness, according to what he calls "vile passions" and a "debased mind" (Romans 1:26, 28). Paul uses sexual ethics and divine biological design to illustrate how far men and women will go to flee from the Lord's wisdom, boundaries and righteousness. What people rage against, ultimately, are the two expressions of God's authority as King and Judge.

If God is seen as a benevolent teacher, however, who kindly gives humanity many choices and ways to engage with Him, and who ultimately gives people the autonomy to govern themselves without any accountability to Him, then all is well in their religious world. In the past, men and women used to get excited about religion when it brought necessary structure to a friend's life, or sobriety to a friend's drunkenness, or peace to a friend's stormy life. But their happiness for a friend's newfound peace included a general ambivalence toward achieving that structure, sobriety or peace themselves. "Getting religion" was fine for someone else, as long as it didn't go beyond that. In their worldview, they were not required to engage with the details of Christian religion and could even be "Christian enough" on their own to live satisfied with their own version of morality.

As Dr. Martyn Lloyd-Jones once said, "The world is as it is tonight because men still think that they can escape the judgment of God."[1]

Paul wrote about this in Romans 2:1–3:

> Therefore you are inexcusable, O man, whoever you are who judge, for in whatever you judge another you condemn yourself; for you who judge practice the same things. But we know that the judgment of God is according to truth against those who practice such things. And do you think this, O man, you who judge those practicing such things, and doing the same, that you will escape the judgment of God?

In other words, by acknowledging that there is a need for justice and judgment on wicked men, humanity cannot claim ignorance of God's goodness and righteousness. There must be a sense of what is right and wrong in order to establish societal boundaries that justify the condemnation of others who are "blatantly evil."

The problem, of course, is that those who are acting as judges see themselves as exempt from the same need for justice and judgment when it comes to their own lives and sins. In their hearts, they do not see themselves as committing the same sin at the same intensity, and therefore they feel they are not subject to the same judgment that others deserve. These are the ones who loudly complain about the sin and lawlessness of others, yet quickly exclaim "Nobody's perfect!" when confronted with sinful areas in their lives. The self-deception that grips the self-righteous heart seeds irrationality into the system—illogical inconsistencies that skillful debate and rational presentations of fact can never penetrate.

If we are confused by the inability of those around us to be rational and civil in disagreement, we must remember that there is an underlying agenda driving much of the present social, civil and political conversation. In an ever-darkening world, more and more people are digging in their heels out of a self-justified sense of someone else's evil and the need for someone else's evil deeds to be stopped and punished. The louder the cries for justice from a sinful, rebellious world, the fiercer the self-justifications become regarding the redefinition of what is sin and what is righteousness. For many, the underlying agenda is to redefine righteousness around "who I am, what I enjoy and what I want to do," with a corresponding redefinition of sin around "what those who oppose me believe." In my zeal, the goal becomes to disempower them from setting cultural, social or civil boundaries of any kind that "oppress" and hinder me from building the kind of world I want to build for myself.

Over the past few decades, we have therefore crossed a threshold. The days of people being glad for others who adopt religion to better their lives have long passed. Now there is a far greater hostility to anyone at all becoming religious. This is rooted in the lust to reshape the world in our own image, and the zeal to remove any possible ideological hindrances to that humanistic end. Yet what should now be very clear to the impartial observer is that humanity has a deep and profound need for religious zeal and fervor. The current political love of the state by the far left and far right (and many in between) is fueled by a neo-religious expression of devotion that has all the pomp and circumstance of High Church ceremony and religiosity. The more fundamentally "religious" even the most hardened atheists and agnostics become about establishing a new, redefined morality, the more zealous they will be about removing all potential competition to this seemingly utopian end.

Why has our society descended into its current expression of redefining sin and raging against Christianity? Ultimately, any who want to see society reshaped according to their own utopian idea need power of all sorts to bring those kinds of systemic changes to their world. Money, resources, influence, political connections, schools and universities, the court system, civil authorities and the police—reordering one's world requires the ability to control and guide these areas according to one's preferred ideology.

Ideological worldview and power are now understood as one reality in the same arena of world building. Christianity is understood as the competing power. This has been the cultural mindset, at least here in the West, since the religious right entered the political arena in the 1980s. Perhaps it is coincidental that the era in which the Church desired to see her worldview expressed in the broader world around her corresponded with the world's sudden and accelerated descent into madness and lawlessness. Whatever the underlying reasons for the collisions with culture that are now taking place within and around the Church, the journey of humanity that began centuries ago has entered another very dark and very troubling phase.

Humanity's Choice and God's Response

Again, the journey itself into greater darkness is not new. We are experiencing the end of a very long journey away from God, and the logical consequences of powerful men shifting society to reflect where their hearts have been for many millennia. Why is there a current acceleration? The era we have entered involves a new level of societal permission for the wealthy and powerful to spend their wealth and express their power in whatever manner they see fit. There has been, in past eras of history, a frustrating boundary set against the base desires of powerful and influential leaders, artists and philosophers who wanted the walls and boundaries of societal permission and resistance to be fully removed. In their generations, they had to settle for a mere chipping away at the cultural and spiritual sensibilities of their world.

From the beginning in the Garden, humanity has had two means available to acquire power: via life from the Father, or via knowledge apart from Him. In my observation, the great besetting sin of this current season is how so many—within the Church and outside the Church—have settled for the knowledge of good and evil as an answer to our powerlessness in the face of evil and injustice. The knowledge of good and evil makes us more aware of what's going on in the world, but it doesn't make us alive or righteous in God. The reason "knowledge puffs up" is because it adds fuel to the fire I spoke of earlier, by which sinful men become more aware of the sin and shortcomings of others (1 Corinthians 8:1). Then in self-delusion they use that increased knowledge to exaggerate how bad others are, heightening their discontent and sense of helplessness because of those they consider inept, incapable and unworthy of the power wielded over them. Humanity wants more than autonomy from God and His authority; ultimately, people want autonomy from other people, deeming them incapable and unworthy of rule. The only ones that stubborn, self-deceived, rebellious people view as worthy of rule are themselves.

On that fateful day of the fall of mankind in our ancient past, humanity made a choice between life with God—and all the blessing, favor, joy and beauty that came with it— and self-governance and autonomy from God. We chose to attempt to build a world that reflected our own sense of beauty, establishing our own version of His blessing and presence. Many millennia later, I am still stunned by what Paul called "the mystery of iniquity" (2 Thessalonians 2:7 KJV). Humanity had been set within the Garden of perfection, beauty and pleasure—the most joy-filled place to commune with our beautiful God, of whom King David sang, "In Your presence is fullness of joy; at Your right hand are pleasures forevermore" (Psalm 16:11). How, then, could it be that humankind could make the fateful choice to cast off God's leadership, authority and beauty and decide that we could build a better world?

It is important to remember that this mystery of humanity's arrogance in the face of God's perfection, absolute wisdom and righteousness still is at work in us. Our stubborn insistence on our own autonomy apart from God—coveting the blessing that comes with His presence but not obeying His boundaries or leadership—all that blindness and self-deception worked in me. It was alive and well within my soul, and at times it still vies for attention in my impatience and unsettled areas of discontentment.

Yet God, the Father of mercies, who is kinder and more tender than I could ever truly grasp, did not start over again with me or any within broken humanity that rejected Him utterly. He did not look to create a new and different version of the first of our kind. He endured for the sake of love. He remained committed to win humanity back, to convince people to surrender their foolish ways voluntarily and yield to His superior pleasures and beauty in the war to build this world. He chose the slow way to win people's hearts, longing to dwell with us forever rather than destroy us outright. His incomparable love that suffers long for sinful, rebellious human beings is so beautiful.

One might ask, "What about the flood of Noah's day?" To some, it might seem as if God did in fact "start over again" with Noah and his family. This kind of conclusion misses a few key points from the narrative. First, Peter called Noah "a preacher of righteousness" (2 Peter 2:5). Noah's labors—for 120 years—bore witness to a coming destructive flood. That generation had 120 years to respond to the Maker of heaven and earth and His appointed vessel of mercy, yet the people refused to believe or repent. Therefore, the second key point to understand is that God preserved any—and in that generation, all—who would respond to His merciful appeal. The final key observation from the narrative is that, like Adam and Eve before them, Noah and his family were still representatives of a fallen race whom God had not given up on. Noah's small family represented hope for the human race—hope for a glorious future, reconciled to God through Christ rather than cast aside as failed and fallen.

The "case" that God will plead with humanity in the future—His contention with us and our contention with Him—involves His right, ability and capacity to rule. There is an element to God's patience and tenderness in pleading His case that offends the sensibilities. Why does it offend us? Because we struggle to comprehend His incomparable power and majesty being expressed through His heart of lowliness and humility. The way He wields His unlimited power as the one with all authority, as the fierce and zealous God of holiness, absolutely demonstrates how our God refuses to be Zeus. He refuses to be reduced to petulant, humanlike wrath at being spurned or disrespected, and He spurns smashing the peoples with nature's wrath until they submit to the higher power confronting them. There will come a time for the finality of God's wrath being poured out in fullness on those who are fully hardened against Him. It will not look like the wrath of Zeus or the wrath of mankind. The God who is slow to anger will shake the mountains in His zeal for

His people, and He will destroy all the demonic, reprobate enemies of His Gospel and goodness.

The Lord does express His wrath as a means of preserving His people and saving humanity from itself when every other means to win human hearts has been exhausted. In Scripture's prophetic books, God expressed His wrath against His enemies when they set their will against all that was good and declared war, and when their unrepentant intentions set in motion their self-destruction, the destruction of the earth and the ravaging of God's people. At the end of the age, when God has attempted every means to plead His case with humanity, and when His enemies still choose a world without Him and His people, He will not be passive as the Father of His family and the Bridegroom of His Bride. We can be assured, however, that even in that day, the full measure of His wrath will be beautiful. Revelation 15 prophesies the deep loyalty and affection of the people of God as they rejoice in His judgments on that day:

They sing the song of Moses, the servant of God, and the song of the Lamb, saying:

> "Great and marvelous are Your works,
> Lord God Almighty!
> Just and true are Your ways,
> O King of the saints!
> Who shall not fear You, O Lord, and glorify Your name?
> For You alone are holy.
> For all nations shall come and worship before You,
> For Your judgments have been manifested."

Revelation 15:3–4

I believe that the "song of the Lamb" is the Song of Solomon itself, the song of God's incomparable love and zeal for His Bride. There will be no followers of Jesus in that day who will find His judgments extreme or unreasonable. No one who knows Him will accuse Him of going too far in His wrath. Why? In the days to come, the saints around the world will have witnessed and participated in the process as the Father was pleading His case patiently with all of humanity.

The way He will plead His case involves the beautification of His Church as His gift to the wicked, that they might see and repent—and relent from doing harm. All the saints will witness and fully express God's unrelenting kindness, and His extravagant patience and mercy. The entire Church—on earth and in heaven—will therefore see with their own eyes the lengths He will go to, to see His enemies and theirs turn and receive His great love.

Before that final day of judgment, the God who offered up His Son for the sake of the world will in turn offer His Son's Bride, the Church. Her members will lay their lives down willingly for their enemies, as if they were friends. The Church will demonstrate the greatest love ever witnessed in order to see the nations turn and be saved. Many, many hearts will come to the knowledge of God in that day. The witness of the beauty of God, expressed through the loving service, selflessness and sacrifice of the end-time Church, will be stunning to behold.

Many have prophesied about a "billion-soul harvest" coming into the Kingdom in the days ahead. I believe that it will be in this context that the largest revival in Church history will sweep across the world. The radical, powerful, accelerated transformation of newly saved saints in that hour, and the quality of their salvation—due in part to the quality of the Church family and community they are being saved into—will be breathtaking and moving.

Yet many will reject this glorious witness. As in the days of the Garden, many will see the beauty of God unveiled in a historically incomparable way through the fullness of the Church in her mature love and Holy Spirit power and authority. Yet they will still rage and reject the Gospel witness, and they will still spurn the loving hand of God, fully extended to them in kindness through His people.

Humanity's Accusation against God

To better understand what is at stake in the conflict between God and humanity, let's examine the nature and depth of the accusation against God. What was the core issue in the Garden and beyond that inspired humankind to make the fateful choice to sin against the Lord and reject His leadership? A delusion is operating within the hearts of all humanity, a delusion about God and about ourselves. Men and women were born with a desire to ascend, to reach the heights of the heavens and express the fullness of human potential. The delusional thinking clouds and distorts this ache when we imagine that we can ascend higher than God in perfection and potential, and therefore we have no need of Him. The ungodliness and unrighteousness of humanity sees God as dispensable— useful if He blesses us and helps us build the world we desire to build, if He serves our will. Humanity therefore desires ascent, but also desires that God would descend.

The unconscious sense of our superiority to God—that our way is better, that our wisdom is superior, and that therefore we have the right to establish our own society and boundaries without His help—is paired with something far more insidious. It is this other element of our rebellion that strengthens and fuels it. It empowers our self-righteousness and self-justification. It emboldens young men and women to walk away from God after reading His words. It strengthens our resolve to resist His counsel and cling to our foolish, darkened ways.

What is this cancer that rots the interior of our soul? At our core, humanity has a case against God built from an accusation against Him. This accusation is not related to what He has or has not done; it is darker and runs deeper. Our collective accusation against the God of Israel is against His character and the core of who He is or claims to be.

At one of the most critical moments in Israel's story, which is also our story of redemption after our very tragic fall, Moses has ascended the mountain of the Lord at Sinai and had looked to discover the essence of who and what God truly is. It is in Exodus 33 and 34 that an exchange happens between God and Moses, and it is one of the most significant conversations in all recorded history between a human being and Yahweh, God of Israel, Creator of heaven and earth. Moses wants to peer beyond the veil between God and humanity, beyond the fire, smoke and light that shrouded God and His holy presence. Yahweh, God of Israel, existed beyond the whirlwind and storm of protective layers that enabled sinful man to approach His sinless, holy presence. Moses longs for intimacy with his

God, the deliverer of Israel from the bondage of Egypt. He longs truly to know Him, and according to the reach of true intimacy, to look upon His face and into His eyes. In those days (and I believe also in ours), to see the face of a man, to look into his eyes, was to truly begin to know him and grow in the understanding of his character.

This is what Moses was asking when he cried, "Please, show me Your glory!" (Exodus 33:18). He was asking the Lord to remove the veil, that he might see Him face-to-face. This was impossible at the time—the cost of a holy God dwelling with sinful man without protective measures set into place was far too great. If God had granted Moses' request, Moses would have been destroyed. As God told him, "You cannot see My face; for no man shall see Me, and live" (verse 20). What God was able to do at that time in history, however, in answering the cry of Moses' heart to know Him without destroying the man in the process, was to give Moses the most intimate, tender answer possible as He passed by him in glory: Yahweh, God of Israel, shared with Moses His name:

> Now the LORD descended in the cloud and stood with him there, and proclaimed the name of the LORD. And the LORD passed before him and proclaimed, "The LORD, the LORD God, merciful and gracious, longsuffering, and abounding in goodness and truth, keeping mercy for thousands, forgiving iniquity and transgression and sin, by no means clearing the guilty, visiting the iniquity of the fathers upon the children and the children's children to the third and the fourth generation."
>
> Exodus 34:5–7

As Yahweh proclaims this to Moses, He is revealing the way He desires to be known and understood—this is the essence of His character and who He is. Twice He uses the word *hesed*, one of the Hebrew words for love, to proclaim His faithful, loyal love for His people, expressed through His lovingkindness and outrageous mercy and patience. Yahweh, God of Israel, our Father who gave us His Son Jesus, is abounding—abounding—in *hesed*. He is overflowing with it, possessing more than enough to fight for us in our wayward, immature foolishness and loveless-ness. When we speak of God contending with humanity to answer the accusation against Him, we are speaking of His desire to convince every man, woman and child ever born that this is who He really is, and that this is who He wants to be, with us and the world He shares with us together, forever.

Yet the accusation within the hearts of humanity—again, the "mystery of iniquity"—is the lust of mankind to declare that Yahweh is *not* these things, and that in fact His character is deceptive and untrustworthy. We accuse Him of being angry and capricious, outdated in morality and ultimately an unworthy ruler of heaven and earth. Within every human soul is such a case we have built against God, all for the purpose of establishing our superiority to Him and liberty from Him. We have an agenda, which is the very core of what "lust" is, and that agenda makes us delusional in our zeal to be right and be above judgment regarding the path we have chosen to take and the choices we continue to make along that path. Humanity apart from God is on a long descent into madness and rage, with so many human hearts exulting in their new boundaries and redefined morality.

Yet God, unyieldingly who He says that He is, is abounding in mercy and slow to anger. He persists in making His case to humanity, insisting on vindicating His name and winning the hearts of His accusers.

By the time His plans are finished, every accusation against Him will have been cast down. At the very end, every objection of humanity will have been answered, and God will be fully vindicated. Although many will still despise Him, every knee will bow, and every tongue will confess that Jesus Christ is Lord (see Philippians 2:10–11).

8

The Vindication of the Name of the Lord

While we are currently living the story of the redemption of humanity, our redemption and transformation are part of an eternal story. We are living and enjoying God's story, which stands far above us all in glory and transcendence. Yet by His will, His story profoundly involves His Church. Repeatedly throughout the Law and the Prophets, the Lord spoke to His people about what He was doing in their generation and in future generations, and why He was acting in the manner that He was. Time and again, He would emphasize that what He did, He did "for the sake of His Name":

> Therefore say to the house of Israel, "Thus says the Lord GOD: 'I do not do this for your sake, O house of Israel, but for My holy name's sake, which you have profaned

among the nations wherever you went. And I will sanctify My great name, which has been profaned among the nations, which you have profaned in their midst; and the nations shall know that I am the LORD,' says the Lord GOD, 'when I am hallowed in you before their eyes.'"

Ezekiel 36:22–23

The plan of God for Israel and all the nations of the earth is profoundly connected to how all the peoples of the earth understand God's name, meaning His character and reputation (as we saw in the last chapter). How God treats, loves, cares for, transforms and restores Israel is a statement or testimony about who He really is and what He is really like. So is how He deals with, serves and forgives His Church as He brings us into our fullness and destiny, and so are all His dealings and interactions with His people. What this oracle from Ezekiel reveals is that God's reputation amongst the nations is synonymous with the actions and character of His people.

This is reemphasized in many other passages of Scripture. It is not only true of Israel, with whom His name was most associated in the ancient world (and will be again in the future), but it is also true of His Church. The outside observers of our faith, as they think about the Church, also think similarly about our God. The apostle Paul emphasized this in his letter to the Romans:

You, therefore, who teach another, do you not teach yourself? You who preach that a man should not steal, do you steal? You who say, "Do not commit adultery," do you commit adultery? You who abhor idols, do you rob

temples? You who make your boast in the law, do you
dishonor God through breaking the law? For "the name of
God is blasphemed among the Gentiles because of you,"
as it is written.

Romans 2:21–24

What is stunning about the Lord is that He chose this
way to relate with the nations of the earth. The humility
and kindness of making covenant with His people par-
tially involves the way that God attaches His name to ours,
but also involves our name and reputation attaching to
Himself. He is fully given to and invested in His people,
partly because of the fact that His very reputation is at
stake amongst all those who are observing and making
judgments about Him based on the quality of His people's
lives and relationships.

We are to be living witnesses, which means that God
wants to show the nations something about Himself
through our lives and stories. We are to give a testimony,
which means that we are testifying before the court of
public opinion that God is who He says He is and will do
all that He has promised. Through His work in us and
our response to His grace, God fashions a powerful case
to answer the accusation of all humanity for all time.

There are some believers with a high view of God
and His sovereignty—and this is a right and biblical
view—who would be confused and offended by the idea
of a God who would stoop so low as to plead His case
with humanity. After all, God answers to no man, which
seems to be part of Isaiah's oracle in proclaiming God's
superiority:

Who has directed the Spirit of the LORD,
Or as His counselor has taught Him?
With whom did He take counsel, and who
    instructed Him,
And taught Him in the path of justice?
Who taught Him knowledge,
And showed Him the way of understanding?

Isaiah 40:13–14

The answer to the dilemma of God's high sovereignty and majesty is found in part by beholding His incomparable humility and meekness, as Paul wrote about in his letter to the Philippians:

> Let this mind be in you which was also in Christ Jesus, who, being in the form of God, did not consider it robbery to be equal with God, but made Himself of no reputation, taking the form of a bondservant, and coming in the likeness of men. And being found in appearance as a man, He humbled Himself and became obedient to the point of death, even the death of the cross. Therefore God also has highly exalted Him and given Him the name which is above every name, that at the name of Jesus every knee should bow, of those in heaven, and of those on earth, and of those under the earth, and that every tongue should confess that Jesus Christ is Lord, to the glory of God the Father.

Philippians 2:5–11

The beauty of God is that He is the one who is sovereign and mighty, transcendent in power, answerable to no one, absolutely and unquestionably righteous and just . . .

and completely secure within Himself regarding His own character and name. He does not need to prove anything to anyone, nor does He need to be vindicated before His accusers and enemies. Yet His deep love for the lost fueled a willingness in Him to draw near to us in our time of greatest need. Drawing near to a people who could not ascend to Him in their own holiness and power, who could not cleanse or justify themselves, therefore required Him to stoop lower than we could ever grasp to pursue us and win our hearts, secure our lives and cultivate our friendship. The entire story of our salvation and redemption is a story filled with the humility and voluntary lowliness of God.

I want to submit a very, very important theme throughout Scripture for us to consider when we seek to understand what motivates the Father in His leadership over our lives and in the way He leads us with great humility and restraint. All the Father does, as it relates to His people and how He leads us, is to the end of producing wholehearted, voluntary love from our hearts toward Him. The restraint, care and skill He exercises in bringing us by grace into wholehearted love, which we choose of our own free will, is another element of His beauty that will leave us stunned for all eternity.

God is looking for obedience to His commands, yes, but obedience from a place of deep agreement with Him. Our agreement causes us to volunteer willingly to serve Him and those He cares for, without holding back. He is looking for something more than a sense of duty; He wants His beauty to produce people motivated by deep desire and their moved hearts.

The Centrality of the Knowledge of God

There are two other key ideas to consider when we're wrestling with the servant-heartedness of God and His humility in fastening Himself, His name and His reputation to Israel and His Church. The first key idea we must understand is that God highly values the impartation of the knowledge of Himself (who He is, what He is like and what we can be confident He will do) to His people. This impartation is the most critical way that we are made rich in Him. The knowledge of God powerfully transforms us and brings us alive in voluntary love, which empowers us to do our part in reaching for more of Him and His personality, presence and power. Without the knowledge of God as our primary pursuit, there is no growth in "first and great commandment" love, mature obedience or a vibrant faith with a burning heart.

A. W. Tozer once wrote this:

What comes into our minds when we think about God is the most important thing about us. The history of mankind will probably show that no people has ever risen above its religion, and man's spiritual history will positively demonstrate that no religion has ever been greater than its idea of God. Worship is pure or base as the worshiper entertains high or low thoughts of God. For this reason the gravest question before the Church is always God Himself, and the most portentous fact about any man is not what he at a given time may say or do, but what he in his deep heart conceives God to be like. We tend by a secret law of the soul to move toward our mental image of God. This is true not only of the individual Christian, but of the company of Christians that composes the Church. Always the most revealing thing about the Church is her idea of God.[1]

What the Father understands is that the knowledge of Him is the ultimate reality that the human spirit can experience in this age and in the age to come. The Church in the days to come will have a vision to go deep in the knowledge of God and will intercede for the release of revelation, until all who love God receive the anointing to make known the riches of Jesus to others (see Ephesians 4:13; 1:17; 3:8). This makes the issue of God's reputation and how He is understood central to His plans and purposes. When we understand the centrality of the knowledge of God to the human experience, we understand His zeal for His name and the way the earth understands Him. God is going to vindicate His name by answering every accusation against Him from the hearts of all humanity, but He is also going to establish the right view of who He is, leaving no doubt or hesitation regarding His just, righteous and merciful nature.

If the Church is powerless, corrupt in character or as ugly in her relationships as is the world, then the nations are free to dismiss our God in the same manner that the ancient world used Israel's impotency as a means of dismissing Yahweh and His prophets. The Gospel loses a measure of its potency, and its appeal diminishes, where there seems little differentiation between secular society and spiritual community, apart from a few objectionable viewpoints on morality. However, something very different happens when the Church is revived and alive in the power of the Holy Spirit. When the Church reflects the holiness and majesty of God, and the lovingkindness and mercy that reflect who Jesus is, the world is forced to align with a very different understanding of the God of Israel.

Beauty Expressed to and through His People

The second key idea for us to consider when we're wrestling with God's humility is the way that God imparts to us the knowledge of who He is. It is important to understand the way that He works according to the "spirit of wisdom and revelation" to help us see what we are mostly blind to in our fallenness, self-centeredness, dullness and pride (Ephesians 1:17; see also verses 18–19). He reveals what cannot be perceived or understood without the help of His grace.

No intelligence or human wisdom can perceive the mysteries of God and His personality and character. We need divine help to perceive Him. Yet we also need help to comprehend and intimately experience that which the Spirit reveals by grace. We need help to see and understand what the Word of God says about God. We know this is true today, but some are shocked to discover that *this will always be true*. We will always face the limitations of our humanity in fully comprehending a transcendent, eternal, infinite Being who exists far, far beyond our ability and capacity ever to grasp, even in the age to come. We will forever marvel in awe and wonder at the beauty, majesty and glory of God. We will forever grow and increase in our understanding and knowledge of Him.

How does a God who is beyond our comprehension and capacity to know and understand bridge that chasm? How does He bring us into the knowledge of Himself? The priestly ministry of Israel was our first glimpse in the ancient world into how God expresses Himself *to* a people so that He can express Himself *through* a people. The priests were to feed on the knowledge of God and then feed the people from their life in the Scriptures and the cultivation of Yahweh's presence in the tabernacle. The result was to be a "kingdom of priests" who served as a "light to the Gentiles," putting Yahweh's goodness and mercy on display for the surrounding nations, as well as for all who passed through her borders (see Isaiah 61:6).

This is part of Israel's "irrevocable calling" that Paul wrote about in Romans 11:29, which means that this promise in Isaiah 60:1–5 is still part of Israel's future:

> Arise, shine;
> For your light has come!
> And the glory of the Lord is risen upon you.
> For behold, the darkness shall cover the earth,
> And deep darkness the people;
> But the Lord will arise over you,
> And His glory will be seen upon you.
> The Gentiles shall come to your light,
> And kings to the brightness of your rising.
>
> Lift up your eyes all around, and see:
> They all gather together, they come to you;
> Your sons shall come from afar,
> And your daughters shall be nursed at your side.

Then you shall see and become radiant,
And your heart shall swell with joy;
Because the abundance of the sea shall be turned
     to you,
The wealth of the Gentiles shall come to you.

This is also, as is the theme of this book, the destiny of the Church. What God promised to Israel will be expressed in the age to come in a way that will be unique to Israel, but not limited to her. The Church has been covenantally included in God's plan to express His beauty and majesty through His people to the earth. In a time of great darkness that covers the earth in our future, we can be assured of God's promise of great light on His people. The Church will humbly seek to "feed" the knowledge of God in one of the darkest hours of history to any who would have ears to hear.

The priestly calling of the Church—to minister to God and to intercede for the people—will be expressed powerfully in this dark time of trouble on the earth. This is why the apostle Peter spoke of our priestly calling as followers of Jesus, and why John the Beloved spoke of the saints being made "kings and priests to our God"—because we have been given the same invitation to be representatives of another Kingdom and our glorious King (see 1 Peter 2:9; Revelation 1:6). As we "feed" on the knowledge of God and in turn serve as "joints of supply" to one another according to that same knowledge, as a people we allow our "light to shine before men" (see Ephesians 4:16; Matthew 5:16; Philippians 2:15).

The ultimate picture of how God expresses what is inexpressible to us in our small, weak, limited humanity is through the Word, the Second Person of the Trinity. God became flesh for more than the remission of our sin; Jesus became Man so that He could express Himself in a way that we could comprehend. He is "the express image" of "the invisible God" and the one who gives voice and human expression to the deep thoughts, desires and plans of the Father's heart (Hebrews 1:3; Colossians 1:15). The Father chose Jesus to speak His thoughts and thus bring them into existence in the natural world under His authority. Jesus is the Word that was with God the Father and the Holy Spirit from the beginning, the Three powerfully unified as the Godhead to bring forth the creation of all things.

For all of humanity—those who are in Christ now and in the age to come—Jesus from the Scriptures, by the indwelling Holy Spirit, and as a man, forever expresses the beauty of the Father to us all. The Holy Spirit exalts Jesus, that through Him we might know the Father, who is "dwelling in unapproachable light" as Paul wrote, "whom no man has seen or can see" (1 Timothy 6:16). When Jesus stated that "no one comes to the Father except through Me," He was speaking of more than our modern evangelical definition of salvation in Christ alone; He was speaking of the very means by which we might know the Father (John 14:6). Our knowledge of God (to the full measure of what, in our limited frame, we can know) is only possible through knowledge of the Son of God. The beauty that God possesses, the Son perfectly expresses, that the Holy Spirit might impart that same beauty to us.

God's Triumph over His Accusers

Paul wrote about the great mystery of the vindication of the Lord's name in Ephesians 3:8–11:

> To me . . . this grace was given, that I should preach among the Gentiles the unsearchable riches of Christ, and to make all see what is the fellowship of the mystery, which from the beginning of the ages has been hidden in God who created all things through Jesus Christ; to the intent that now the manifold wisdom of God might be made known by the church to the principalities and powers in the heavenly places, according to the eternal purpose which He accomplished in Christ Jesus our Lord.

What is this mystery Paul spoke about, which was hidden in ages past but now is being declared openly? Paul continues in verses 14–19:

> For this reason I bow my knees to the Father of our Lord Jesus Christ . . . that He would grant you, according to the riches of His glory, to be strengthened with might through His Spirit in the inner man, that Christ may dwell in your hearts through faith; that you, being rooted and grounded in love, may be able to comprehend with all the saints what is the width and length and depth and height—to know the love of Christ which passes knowledge; that you may be filled with all the fullness of God.

I know we examined this passage in a couple of earlier chapters, yet there are layers within it that are helpful for us to "peel back" as we grow in our understanding of the treasures that await us in the heart of God. Paul's prayer is that the saints of God would be exhilarated by the "riches of His glory," that the One who dwells within us by the Holy Spirit would empower us to be filled with the fullness of His love. Paul's desire was that the entire Body of Christ worldwide—together "with all the saints"—would know the fullness of experiencing and expressing the beauty and love of Jesus.

This is how the manifold wisdom of God will be made known to all, when they see the quality, depth and selfless, mature love of the saints for Jesus, for one another and for the lost. The revival that is coming will be a revival that goes beyond power for the lost to come to Jesus, or power for signs and wonders. It will include these things, but a much more powerful expression of God's power is coming to the Church. It will be a full deliverance from the present lukewarm, half-hearted doublemindedness and immaturity, and it will bring the fullness of the love of God as a final gift to a darkening world at the height of its accusation against God and His Son. It will be, as my dear friend Mike Bickle calls it, "the greatest social miracle in all of human history." The saints of the end-time Church will be delivered into the fullness of Paul's prayer in one of the most stunning turnarounds the earth has ever seen.

The Church is presently divided, carnal-minded, immature and lukewarm, with seemingly irreconcilable ideological gaps, and pain that at times seems beyond healing, and with wounded relationships that seem beyond reconciliation. The Western Church specifically seems to be at war with itself, but this is not the end of our story. The Lord has a solution borne of intercession and the stirring of His Holy Spirit. Long before He revives and dramatically transforms His Church, He is awakening an ache of dissatisfaction and discontentment in the hearts of many saints around the world. The Father is not waiting for tomorrow's deliverance; He is beginning to work in hearts and lives today. The future of the Church begins *now* for the repentant, for those who are profoundly dissatisfied with their own relationship with the Lord and who find no comfort in carnal definitions of success or in comparing their spirituality to others in their relational sphere.

Our deliverance from a lukewarm spirit begins with an honest dialogue with the Lord about our lukewarmness. If we never ask the Lord, *Am I lukewarm?*, we become content never to know. Instead, we busy ourselves with cultural distractions that help us ignore the underlying ache in us for more of the beauty of God. If we ask Him, however, then a divine escort into the fullness of what we were made for begins in us with a reawakened longing that only God can stir up. Without shame, we can acknowledge our current condition and ignore the noise of comparison about how we feel others are doing (or not doing). We can ask the Lord for today's provision of the grace to hunger for Him. We can ask Him to help us pursue a renewed fascination with His beauty, the experience of His love and the increase of the knowledge of Him.

This is how the Lord rescues His Church. He does it suddenly—seemingly out of the blue, while the rest of the world has been paying no attention. But when the story is fully told, we realize that He has been stirring His people all along, little by little, one heart here, one discontented soul there. He began, hopefully, with you, with me, and with millions around the world just like us—those of us who want to be free of our lethargy and half-heartedness, to long for more of God, and who want to cast our cares upon Him and see where He takes us by grace. We put our heads down with resolve, and we pursue Him as He draws us away. When we look up, we will find that many millions have gone on the same journey, and suddenly the Church is radiant and bright, beautiful and fierce.

What begins with simple repentance will culminate with a global deliverance and transformation, for the sake of the Lord's name and His great fame around the earth, silencing all accusations against His character in the process.

9

The Fearless Church and the Consummation of Beauty

In Revelation 3:14–21, Jesus addresses the lukewarm church of Laodicea. He gives the way forward for them and for any who would genuinely war to overcome a lukewarm spirit by grace. This is a war Jesus intends to win, as He will not have a half-hearted, distracted, lethargic and disinterested Bride at His return.

The greatest issue for the global Church is a lukewarm love for Jesus. Other competing loves, the continual assault of various fears, the comparison to and mistrust of other Christians, and a losing battle against loneliness and pain are all symptoms of this greater sickness. The issue of lukewarm love is a far greater issue to overcome than any other secondary issue of conflict and difficulty, be it racial tensions, progressive theology, controlling leaders, biblical illiteracy or anything else.

Where there are degrees of lovelessness, half-heartedness or double-mindedness, there are equal measures of fear. As I stated earlier, fear is the great enemy of love. Even spiritual lethargy or boredom with God has its roots in real fears. We might fear that at the end of our race, we could find out that the things we sacrificed, left behind or passed by to pursue God might not ultimately have been worth sacrificing. These hidden fears that propel us daily explain why our spiritual boredom most often leads to busyness more than it does laziness. Our spiritual lethargy does not mean we are tired; it means we are less fascinated with God and more fixated on our lack in other areas. We therefore prioritize those other areas over our area of greatest need, the need to know Him and His beauty.

The ancient fathers of the faith wrote more about spiritual boredom and the lukewarm spirit than anyone. In fact, this was a major subject of their writings for a millennium, up to the days of Thomas Aquinas, who wrote extensively about this subject. One ancient father of the faith, Evagrius, wrote about the spiritual "sloth" he observed in his fellow monks. As one scholar observed about him,

Sloth, for him, may have taken the form of a lack of focus, a persistent refusal to shoulder the self-discipline of his true vocation. If this is true then we can widen the scope of what Evagrius meant by sloth to include the attempts we all make to evade what we really should be doing with our lives. Sloth becomes the pursuit of distraction, the deliberate frittering away of time in the attempt to escape choice and commitment. It means keeping all possibilities endlessly open rather than committing ourselves to a particular task, person or way of life. Evagrius knew that the monk afflicted by acedia will want very much to leave his cell. Evagrius depicts the troubled monk staring at doors, hoping for a visitor, jumping up at every sound and constantly leaning out of the window. He also yawns frequently and drops off readily to sleep; he reads, but cannot concentrate on what he is reading, but turns the pages, leafing through to the end.[1]

It was Saint Thomas Aquinas who wrote about this affliction of the soul being connected to a deep dissatisfaction with the beauty and the love of God. He understood that a wholehearted God who desired unbroken friendship and intimacy with humanity would often be met with an interior sadness on the part of mankind. What is the root of this sadness? Another scholar commented about Aquinas's answer to this,

> If it is quite logical that every agent should act first out of love, then how is it that man can be saddened in the presence of God? And Thomas answers: Man is capable of being sad in the presence of God because for God's sake he must renounce other goods that are carnal, temporal, limited, apparent goods, which on the scale, though, will weigh more than spiritual good, which may seem much less concrete than some particular good that is immediately attainable.[2]

Fear is the underlying issue with our spiritual boredom, our interior lethargy about the extravagant love of God, and our lack of fascination with His beauty. Our underlying fear is borne of our unbelief and a mistaken sense of God's relative worth related to the quality of our life today, in the here and now. It does not always seem practical to us to "waste our lives" in the pursuit of hunger for God, a vibrant spirit, and a tender heart filled with the knowledge of His Word. When we pray, fast, take time in the Word, serve others or give our money to the Kingdom, we might fear that we are constantly missing other opportunities because of those humble acts of weakness in faith. Overcoming a lukewarm spirit begins by acknowledging our genuine dissatisfaction with God and our lack of fascination with Him. Because of our lukewarmness, we are not moved by Him or captured by our knowledge of Him the way we were meant to be.

There is a war raging within our souls, and we often find ourselves allying with the external forces of the world, which are also warring for our attention, passion and desires. It is critical for us to know that this is not an unwinnable war, and in fact Jesus intends to win—utterly eradicating our fears, unbelief and ultimately our own interior accusations against Him in the process.

God's Delight in Delivering His People

Before the Father vindicates His name before the whole world in one generation, He will vindicate His name in the deepest depths of our broken souls. He will remove every hidden accusation against His name, His worth and

His beauty, establishing the supremacy of the victorious Bridegroom who frees our hearts to choose to love Him fully and voluntarily. How will God do this? He will deliver us from both fear and boredom that so we can behold His beauty.

The ancient fathers who wrote about this issue of the lukewarm heart summarized the way forward with one simple word: *perseverance*. In that concept, perseverance, they summarized our part in the struggle to truly overcome spiritual boredom—which, undealt with, could lead to spiritual death. Yet this is not about willing our way into a quality of love for Jesus that we do not have and cannot muster up within ourselves. We can get ourselves into all manner of dilemmas and trouble because of our brokenness, foolishness and what the apostle Peter called our "shortsighted" ways (2 Peter 1:9). We cannot, however, deliver ourselves from the trouble we get into. "God helps those who help themselves" is a humanistic lie that imagines that the universe begins and ends with us, as God helps us along the path. The truth is that Jesus is our source, the only one who can and will save us from ourselves and the sin that so easily entangles us. He is our Deliverer.

As you may recall from an earlier chapter where we talked about God's delight in us despite our weakness, the even better news is that, to paraphrase King David, God delivers us because He delights in us (see 2 Samuel 22:20; Psalm 18:19). Our deliverance is fully in the hands of the One who takes great delight in our lives and in our love, as weak and small as it all is.

This means that we don't need to make another New Year's resolution to "feel God more" or craft a five-step plan to "be more fervent this year." In our production-oriented, bottom line–driven world, well-meaning leadership gurus may be waiting for us just around the corner, ready to deliver action plans to break out of spiritual boredom. But these are not the answers we need. The fathers of our faith had a profound understanding of the practical matters of a vibrant spirituality. They understood the delineation between "our part" and God's role in our lives, and they therefore knew how to persevere. They knew how to endure in the small areas of diligence and faithful obedience, areas that will set our cold hearts before the fiery flame of God's passionate desire and wholehearted love for us.

Perseverance is made possible in part by growing in our understanding of who God is, what He will do, and why He is motivated to do things on our behalf to serve us. All these questions, answered within Scripture, work anew in us to stir up and move our dull, weak hearts and awaken a fresh fascination with God's beautiful, merciful leadership in our lives. That is why the passages in Revelation chapters 2 and 3 that address the early Church's shortcomings, deficiencies or sin do not begin with a rebuke or a command to the churches in question. The failures of those churches are not the first thing Jesus addresses. The first thing He says to each church as He engages the early believers in their areas of compromise is something about Himself. *This is who I am*, He tells them with great authority, passion and tenderness. *This is who I am, in light of what you have done*, He continues, connecting the specific revelation of His beauty with the specific area of their failure. Finally, He says, in summary, *This is who*

I am, in light of what you have done, because this is who you really are to Me.

The question of who those churches were in that era cannot be understood through the lens of the specific issues Jesus was addressing. The bigger story of who they were to Him is implied by His passion and jealousy for their destiny, which motivated Him to address and help them in their specific areas of weakness. Those areas of weakness threatened to rob them of a portion of their inheritance in Him, and He stood in the midst of them to fight for that portion on their behalf—and to win.

I love the picture of Jesus in Revelation chapters 1 through 3. He doesn't stand above or ahead of the stars and lampstands that represent the churches and their leaders. He stands in the midst of the stars and lampstands. He stands joyfully among them, with them and alongside them as the servant of all, there to deliver them from evil.

He stands in the midst of your life, too. He is eager to help you. It delights Him to do so.

This is our confidence—that the One who stands beside us, burning with passion and joy to deliver us, is the One called "the Amen, the Faithful and True Witness, the Beginning of the creation of God" (Revelation 3:14). These are aspects of Jesus' beauty that were specifically chosen to bolster our confidence that deliverance was more than possible, but was a matter of time. The One called in effect "So Be It" in this Scripture, whose name is "Certainty" or "Trustworthy," is standing beside us in our spiritual boredom, with joyful zeal to bring us out of it. The "Amen" is the One who declared on the cross, "It is finished!" Therefore, we can be confident that He will

173

finish what He started with our lives, and with the life of every Christian we know.

Imagine whispering to Jesus, right this very moment, *Jesus . . . all-powerful One . . . You love me . . . I'd like to ask . . . could You, well . . . could You deliver me from my lukewarm spirit?*

If you could hear His reply, you would hear the sound of fiercely clapping thunder, paired with the sound of a coolly refreshing brook in springtime, after the winter thaw. These are the sounds of His joy, paired with His fierce determination to answer your cry. You would hear Him say with all booming authority and confidence, *Consider it done!*

This, beloved, is who He is when He tells us that He is the Amen. He also tells us that He is the Faithful and True Witness, and by that He means more than that He will do all He has promised to do in our lives. The Faithful and True Witness means that if we want to catch a glimpse of what our deliverance from spiritual boredom and a lukewarm heart looks like, we must simply look at how He expresses wholehearted devotion to us. He is not bored with us in any way. He never finds His friendship with us tedious or dull. He never feels cold on the inside toward us or discontented with us because of our fear, unbelief or sense that someone better is out there to love. No! We have a Faithful and True Witness who moves us deeply with His fully given, no holding back, unreserved, fearless love for us. He is not worried about being hurt or rejected by us. He is not guarded. His heart is wide open to us, without any fear about our capacity to be cruel and casual about Him.

It is impossible to ponder and think about even these few facets of God's infinite beauty and be unmoved. If we stop to meditate on the One who is that full of enthusiasm over our friendship with Him, eventually it will overwhelm our weak hearts with gratitude and wonder. He is the living personification of the most beautiful sunset imaginable, the radiant light of His multifaceted love for us washing us and daring us to be disinterested or distracted.

Beloved, there are nineteen other expressions of God's beauty in just these first three chapters of Revelation alone. In addition, there are many, many more facets of His beauty, character, emotions and personality in Revelation chapters 4 and 5. We have to stop and wonder when we realize that there are 22 chapters of this prophetic book entitled "The Revelation [or Unveiling] of Jesus Christ," and here we are, lost in two points of one paragraph of one chapter!

This is where we persevere. We stay with the slow, steady work of reading about God, thinking about God and talking about God. Over time, our cold hearts begin to grow strangely warm as He does the rest of the work in us by grace.

"Be Zealous and Repent"

The reason we need a Faithful and True Witness to show us what fiery, awakened passion for the Father (and for the Church) looks like is because the lukewarm often do not know or perceive that they are lukewarm. We confess that we are rich, and in need of nothing. Yet we are blind, Jesus tells us, and therefore cannot see our true condition, which He describes as wretched, naked and spiritually poor. We would rather rebuke Jesus for His negative confession. We would rather pretend that we didn't hear those words, and continue on as if everything with us was as God intended under the banner of grace and "accepting me as I am." We have come to accept and like ourselves as we are, so why would we want to hear that we are wretched?

If we could see our lukewarm love in the light of God's fearless, open-hearted and joyful givenness to our life together . . . if we could see how enthusiastic He is about awakening our dull hearts to love the way we were made to love . . . if we could see all of this without feeling shame or rejection (even the rejection of ourselves in frustration and prideful perfectionism), we would nod in agreement. We would ask for His help. Most critically, according to Jesus, we would "be zealous and repent" (Revelation 3:19). Zeal would awaken within us when a very simple revelation of His joyful, patient persistence ignited our understanding.

Why would we be zealous and repent? Because "Behold," He cries, "I stand at the door and knock" (verse 20). Our Deliverer is telling us, *I am standing outside the door of your heart, knocking and wanting to come in.*

That's when it hits us: We thought we had become rich and wealthy, and had need of nothing, when suddenly we are lovingly informed of the truly wretched state of our heart and soul (see verse 17). Jesus is on the outside, wanting to come in and be with us.

Here is the beauty of the Lord and His great love. It is in His appeal, which begins, *You who were self-deceived and who let your heart grow bored with Me and My love—I want you to know that I love you as fully and as fiercely as I ever have.* He continues, *And if you will be zealous and repent, you will open to the One who knocks at your door even now.*

Suddenly, our heart begins to move, and maybe, just maybe, the tears begin to flow a little. Jesus is joyfully, faithfully, willingly waiting outside our door, gently knocking to come in, and repentance is as simple as opening the door for Him to enter. Then, with a reach for our hearts so potent that you can almost hear the ache for our love in His voice, He says to the lukewarm, the spiritually bored, the fearfully lethargic, "If anyone hears My voice and opens the door, I will come in to him and dine with him, and he with Me" (Revelation 3:20). From the days of Israel's elders dining with God on Mount Sinai, to the Tabernacle of Moses and the sacrificial meal, to the Last Supper, we find yet again that Jesus longs to share a meal with His closest friends. He is coming with great longing to His dearest friends, asking them to zealously repent of their boredom with Him, and expressing His earnest desire to have a meal with them—with you and with me.

He finishes this passage in Revelation 3 with an appeal to our ultimate destiny with Him (see verse 21). Our place, role and state of being are not meant to be in the same room with Him but at a cold, bored distance, while we occupy our thoughts and restless hearts with trifling distractions and petty busyness. We are His closest, dearest, most treasured friends. Our place is to sit with Him on His throne, to rule with Him. We were made to partner and govern with Him as His Bride. We were made for Him to be our Beloved Bridegroom and dearest Friend.

As you will see at the end of the next chapter, I am more than confident that this is the future of the entire Body of Christ, in one generation, before the Lord's return. I am absolutely certain that the Lord will explode with joy on the day in which all has been set in motion, everything is in its rightful place, and the time is right to deliver His Church fully and completely around the world from our spiritual boredom, dullness and lethargy. We will all be delivered from our lukewarm love, and we will all be delivered into the most fearless, powerful, beautiful expression of love for Jesus and love for one another that the earth has ever seen. When that happens, it will be surprisingly easy for us to love our enemies. Imagine the global Church, before the Lord returns, full of unified, humble hearts working to love, serve, bless and pray for her enemies, regardless of the evil they express toward her. This will be a Church with no complaints or accusations against God or others, filled with gratitude and a heart of mercy. What a miracle of grace!

The lukewarm Church worldwide has a fear problem because it has a love problem. Fear thrives where love is weak. Where love is strong, fear diminishes, and where love is perfected, fear is completely cast aside—"perfect love casts out fear" (1 John 4:18). The Lord is going to deal with our fear, unbelief and distorted sense of His worth by persistently, patiently and repetitively confronting us with His beauty. Over time, and then suddenly and all at once, His beauty will fully conquer the hearts of His people, who will worship from a place of true awestruck wonder, with tears of joy-filled gratitude. They will no longer worship God out of duty or distracted devotion. He will be ours, and we will be His, and our hearts will be alive with love and enjoyment of one another like nothing we have ever experienced.

It will be in the days of our deliverance from the luke-warm spirit that we will learn another surprising and slightly painful truth. We will realize, in the moment of our deliverance, what we missed out on with Jesus. But we will also have a slight moment of regret and sadness when we realize what we missed out on with one another. For when our spirits were lukewarm, our self-absorption and dulled eye for beauty didn't just put a wall and guard up between God and us. It also kept us at arm's length from one another. We were unable truly to see and be moved by the beauty of the other people set into our community as God's magnificent gift to us. Our regret and sadness will quickly pass, however, and we will be free for the first time—almost like waking from a bad dream—to truly see, appreciate, understand, enjoy and freely and fully love our friends and co-laborers.

It will be exhilarating.

And the gift that it will be for us in the time that immediately follows will be absolutely critical if we are to stand in the face of what all of the nations will do to us afterward. We will need to be able to persevere and endure, since the world will hate us for His Name's sake (see Matthew 10:22; 24:9). His love expressed to us and through us as His people, however, will shine forth beyond the darkness of mankind's sin and rage. His love and beauty expressed to us and through us as His Church will be the

Father's light to the world. It will declare to the world the truth of who He really is and what He is really like. The Church at the end of the age will experience the incomparable delight that comes with being filled with love without fear, being wholehearted in devotion, and being able to face the storm with unspeakable joy.

10

The Unshakable Love of the End-Time Church

The centerpiece revelation of the beauty of Jesus in the book of Revelation—which, again, would be best understood as the "Unveiling of Jesus Christ"—is, as a matter of fact, the grand moment of "unveiling" before the throne of God. In the early part of Revelation, Jesus reveals stunning and specifically personal facets of His beauty to the Church steeped in compromise and immaturity. The underlying theme of the first three chapters involves the preparation and transformation of the saints by God's beauty so that the Bride can make herself ready to be presented to Jesus by His Father (see Revelation 19:7).

The apostle John's vision dramatically shifts from this point, changing "locations" from Jesus in the midst of His Church to John himself in the midst of the throne room of heaven. In this shift, we move from the beauty of Jesus to what has been called "the beauty realm of God." In the throne room, the beauty of God's heart and character is on display through an overwhelming mixture of light, color, sounds and fragrance, intermingled with fantastic creatures and simple, melodic angelic choruses. The Father is seen as seated and expressing His sovereign leadership over the earth and all that is about to unfold. This scene is shared with us for the express purpose of fastening our hearts in confidence to the Father's authority and leadership, in light of the hell that will break loose on the earth.

The beauty and order above are a direct contrast to the ugly chaos and brutal lawlessness below that will be part of the "deep darkness" that Isaiah prophesied about (see Isaiah 60:2). In the Father's hand we see the answer to bringing beauty to the earth, removing the ugliness and darkness, and establishing His order, peace and Sabbath rest for all peoples. It is a scroll giving permission to the Man who holds it to unleash corresponding cataclysmic judgments on the enemies of God that will cause them to repent or be removed. Whoever holds the scroll wields unprecedented power over every man, woman and child alive across every nation, tribe and language.

We learn that no man or woman, living or dead, is worthy to take hold of such a scroll, save the One. Only this One from amongst the human race is worthy to stand before Yahweh on His throne, take the scroll from His hand and exercise unprecedented authority over the nations. We know the only One who it could be, the only One worthy to take the scroll and open its seals, unleashing the judgments of God.

Yet when this One is introduced to us, it is as if we are meeting Him for the first time. He is not introduced to us as Jesus of Nazareth, nor is He referred to as the Word. He is introduced as the Hope of Israel, the Messiah, and the Restorer of the Davidic lineage of kings. John looks into and past the whirlwind that Moses could not see beyond. He looks into the storm of light, smoke, fire and glory that had veiled Yahweh from Moses' sight centuries earlier. Here and now, John the Beloved was going to see with his own eyes the answer to the ancient question that Moses had asked, *Show me Your glory!*

John looks into the storm, to the center of the throne, looking to see the Messiah, the Son of David and the Rightful King of Israel. John is now looking at the very center of the universe itself, the source and definition of life itself. From this place and this throne, the very course of the universe itself and all beauty will be defined and set in motion from the seat of God's government in heaven. The entire scene is described as a series of concentric circles expanding infinitely outward from the center circle, the core and centerpiece of the endless room John found himself in. At the center of that stood the Man, the One who would take the scroll, loose the judgments of God and deliver the world from the chaos, brutality and disorder that threatened to devour everything and everyone below. Yet when John looked into the center of the storm, through the whirlwind, he saw something shocking:

> And I looked, and behold, in the midst of the throne and of the four living creatures, and in the midst of the elders, stood a Lamb as though it had been slain, having seven

horns and seven eyes, which are the seven Spirits of God sent out into all the earth. Then He came and took the scroll out of the right hand of Him who sat on the throne.

Revelation 5:6–7

We think of this as purely symbolism, depicting the act of Jesus' death on the cross as the deed that made Him the one worthy to receive the scroll. However, this scene is something much more. At the center of the universe, we find the ultimate expression of Jesus' beauty. This beauty is an expression that is ultimately meant to define who the Church is to become as well. As Christians, we understand the act of Jesus' sacrificial death to be the ultimate statement about who He is, and therefore we focus on the word *slain* in the text more than on the title *Lamb*. Jesus as "the slain Lamb" is meant to be understood as something *more*, however, than the sacrificial act He performed in the past. It reveals who Jesus is at the core of His being, and how He wants to be understood. When it comes to the "Unveiling of Jesus Christ" and how He wants to be known and understood in light of the unprecedented shaking and trouble that is to follow as the rest of the vision unfolds, Jesus wants us to see Him as the Lamb.

It is the Lamb who is worthy to rule, who is worthy to take the scroll and open the seals of judgment. It is the Lamb who then initiates the judgments of God in Revelation 6. He is measured and restrained in the execution of judgment, seeking to shake the earth and get the attention of all its peoples, versus unleashing total destruction on the unrepentant wicked. He desires to be merciful, seeks repentance and is the meekest, most gentle of all. His title is Lion, but He leads in a gentle, lowly, Lamb-like manner. He loves His enemies. He takes no pleasure in the death of the wicked. He desires that none should perish, but that all should come to repentance. He desires that all men be saved and come to the knowledge of God (see Ezekiel 18:23; 33:11 regarding the death of the wicked; 2 Peter 3:9, that none should perish; 1 Timothy 2:4, that all men should be saved).

This is the image that Jesus desires to conform His Church to at the end of the age. We see the center of the throne through John's eyes because we are meant to understand that Jesus' beauty as the slain Lamb will be our beauty as we express who He really is, and what He is really like at the core of His being, to the nations at their most irrational, wicked, lawless and hostile. Jesus was so gentle, composed, at rest and fixed on His prize as He stood before Pilate. Most men broke in that scenario and begged for their life, whimpering with fear at their coming torment. Jesus was not most men, and Pilate was moved, believing that he stood before the true king of Israel, but not realizing that he stood before the willing Lamb who was consenting to lay down His life for His friends.

Unshakable, Unoffendable Love

The end-time Church will be so transformed by Jesus' beauty, so filled with His love, and therefore so fearless and wholehearted, that she will be marked by profound rest and contentment. She will have a tender heart that the world will not be able to steal, trample down or mar in any way. Her unshakable, unoffendable love will come from a heart conquered by God's beauty.

The heart of the Church will be like our Shulamite bride from earlier. The Church will be free of the lukewarm dullness that once robbed her and weighed her down. Her heart will be buoyant, light and filled with joy in the midst of even the darkest of circumstances or bleakest of moments. If one saint has another to share the dark moments with, this means that Jesus is gathered with them in their sweet intimacy and affection for Christ and for one another. To them, this kind of deep fellowship will feel superior to food in that hour. Picture the kindest person you can possibly imagine—the kindest person from your church, your family or someone you met who inspires you to be kind. The entire end-time Church will collectively far surpass the kindness of the man or woman you are thinking of.

As these days approach, I often think about Betsy and Corrie ten Boom, two well-known sisters in a prison camp during World War II. Though many have heard parts of their story and have been inspired by their courage to give shelter and a hiding place to Jews being hunted by the Nazi regime, few people I have spoken with know the details of these sisters' fellowship in the darkness of their prison camp. There, the sweetness of their love for each other and for Jesus was a light in the midst of tormenting darkness. They led secret Bible studies in the midst of oppressive flea infestations. They worked to keep others alive and warm in the oppressive and at times fatal cold. Betsy continually called her sister higher in love and faith, expressing her certain hope that the sisters would minister the love of Jesus to former Nazis after the war. The fire in Betsy's heart, and the way it kept Corrie's heart aflame in those dark hours, so moves and inspires me. I encourage you to reengage with their story when you are able. I believe it is a powerful picture of what the whole Church—every single saint on earth—will look like in the sweet unity of a mature love for Jesus at the end of the age.

Before Jesus' return, in the context of what He described in Matthew 24:10 as unprecedented hatred, betrayal and offense, the Church will shine with a radiant light of unoffendable courage and loyalty. The saints who love Jesus at the end of the age will be faithful to one another and will be incapable of betrayal or hatred, even for the most brutal of their enemies. Imagine engaging at that time as a sinful man or woman who is not in Christ, wondering who will betray you and when it will happen. Imagine never being able to trust anyone to any degree, always looking over your shoulder, never feeling safe, never feeling loved and never daring to love anyone, all in order to protect your heart and life from the brutality of true lawlessness in that hour.

Now imagine such a man or woman finding his or her way into a church community in those days. The contrast would be so impossibly stark as to be unbelievable at first. In the context of unprecedented hatred, betrayal and offense, imagine finding a people willing to love you, serve you, bless you and even forgive you and show mercy if and when you betray them. They will be shrewd as serpents, but always gentle as doves and eager to express the love Jesus has set within them. For many of the lost, it will feel like coming home. It is not hard to believe in such an hour that billions will repent and be saved into that kind of love and beauty.

Days of War and Triumph

Those days to come will see both war against the Lamb and the triumph of the saints. Many passages of Scripture give a clear picture of messengers taking the Gospel of the Kingdom to the ends of the earth. The lost will find the love of Jesus in spiritual families around the world, but messengers of the Kingdom will also go in teams to the ends of the earth to find the lost. At that time, every single person on earth will hear about the Good News of the coming Kingdom of God and have an opportunity to repent and be saved.

Kings, generals, wealthy and powerful businessmen, slaves, the weak and the lowly of the earth—all will hear the Gospel message, with the power of the Holy Spirit testifying to the truth of the message. Many, many people from everywhere will see the healing power of the Holy Spirit, as well as many other signs, wonders and miracles. The merciful offer God will make to all peoples at that time will be like no other time in history. At what other time in any generation has there ever been that kind of Gospel preaching, accompanied by historic signs and wonders far beyond the book of Acts or the book of Exodus, along with the collective global witness of the transformed end-time Church? (See Revelation 11's two witnesses or Revelation 16's bowl judgments for pertinent examples of this statement.)

The great shock of that time will be the capacity of the wicked to grow darker in their wickedness, even in the face of God's historic expression of mercy and kindness. The answer of the powerful, of those who despise God and refuse to turn from their sins of murder, theft, sexual immorality and sorcery, will be to declare war on the Lamb and on His people (see Revelation 9:21). God will raise up the kindest, most gentle, most loving and forgiving people that the earth has ever seen, and the powerful and unrepentant will do to the Church what their fathers did to Jesus many centuries ago. It was shocking when they put Jesus to death, and at the end of the age they will seek to do the same to His Bride.

By the actions of both groups, the Father's name will be vindicated, fully cleared of all charges and accusations against Him, and He will be fully exonerated in His character and actions. The quality and depth of godly character in the Church, her meekness and humility, her unshakable and unoffendable love and mercy in that day, will be a powerful testimony and witness to the nature of the God we worship and what His grace and love can produce in the weak and the broken who yield to His loving leadership.

At the same time, God's accusers will indict themselves through their brutality and beastlike rage against the saints. Those who are condemned to perish will condemn themselves and render their accusations against God meaningless by the way that they treat the saints; they will be "drunk with the blood of the saints and with the blood of the martyrs" (Revelation 17:6). All peoples from all nations will clearly see two kingdoms and the vast difference between the two as the Kingdom of God shines brightly in the midst of the fullness of humanity's darkness.

One of the most powerful statements about the end-time Church is proclaimed in Revelation 12:10–11:

> Then I heard a loud voice saying in heaven, "Now salvation, and strength, and the kingdom of our God, and the power of His Christ have come, for the accuser of our brethren, who accused them before our God day and night, has been cast down. And they overcame him by the blood of the Lamb and by the word of their testimony, and they did not love their lives to the death."

Not only will there be no accusation against God in that day, since the actions of both the saints and the wicked will fully vindicate His name. There will also be no accusation against the saints! The brightness of the spotless, blameless Bride of Christ in that hour will be such that even Satan himself will have no inroads to accuse her. This is the promise of Ephesians 5:25–27:

> Husbands, love your wives, just as Christ also loved the church and gave Himself for her, that He might sanctify and cleanse her with the washing of water by the word, that He might present her to Himself a glorious church, not having spot or wrinkle or any such thing, but that she should be holy and without blemish.

The future of the Church is glorious. She will be filled with beauty and will triumph over all her enemies, even as she forgives and loves many of them into salvation. The Church will serve to vindicate the Lord's name and reputation, silencing His accusers and displaying His heart and goodness. In the process, the Lord will vindicate her before all of her accusers who hold her in contempt. The story of the Church is going to be turned completely upside down, and she will be sanctified, cleansed, holy and without blemish.

It will be her finest hour. In that day, we will marvel, awestruck with wonder, and be forever filled with gratitude for the Lord who did such a sign and a wonder. We will taste a measure of the sweetness of the age to come here, on earth, prior to the return of Jesus and the end of the age. We will enter into the next age with much celebration of God and His Son, and of the saints we were blessed to serve alongside, "the excellent ones, in whom is all my delight" (as David said in Psalm 16:3).

I personally cannot wait to live that story. I long to see that day with my natural eyes and enjoy it all with my children and their children. Until then, it is my task and yours to prepare ourselves and them for that day. Maranatha!

CONCLUSION

The Love of the Godhead Fully Expressed by the Church

Perhaps you have been a bit thrown off by the confidence and certainty of my presentation and conclusions about the future of the Church. From where do I derive that level of certainty about the future? Are the elements of the future described in Scripture open to various interpretations?

My starting point in building my understanding of the Church's future—and therefore, of my future and yours, and the future of the next generation—is not in prophecy, but in a prayer. The apostolic prayers are a powerful expression of hope related to the future of the Church. The prayers of Paul alone might be enough to instill within us an unshakable confidence in the plans of God to escort His Church into her fullness and great beauty. It is the prayer of Jesus Himself in John 17, however, that provides me with a "base of understanding" to work from in building my presentation of what Scripture describes as the victorious Church at the end of the age.

One place in Scripture that helps us grow in our understanding of a future victorious Church is found in the "Upper Room Discourse" of John 13–17. What Jesus shares in these chapters is incredibly powerful. It is almost a singularly stabilizing force to serve the troubled or unsettled heart in the face of grave disruption, betrayal and great heartache. As I discussed in an earlier chapter, on the eve of His own death, Jesus takes the time to wash, pastor and express profound love for His friends on the eve of their own "dark night" moment. Jesus gives them the perspective, critical instruction and call to engage the power of the Holy Spirit to cultivate the depths of love, pleasure and joy available to the human heart. To go the way Jesus prescribes is to cultivate an "untouchable heart" that has bought the "gold refined in the fire" from Revelation 3, which Jesus counseled the lukewarm to buy (verse 18).

The entire Upper Room Discourse is best understood in an end-time context of ultimate shaking and unprecedented trouble. In these passages, Jesus gives us the way to a fiery seal of divine love that is stronger than the grave, and that many waters cannot quench (see Song of Solomon 8:6–7). In His words in these discourse chapters, Jesus offers a way to lay hold of the kind of love that is far stronger than the intense, tragic and difficult events that will shape the final years of this age before He returns.

By the time Jesus comes to His own prayer—for Himself, for His friends and for His Church—He prays and asks the Father to set His Church into the kind of quality of love that is far beyond what any saint would imagine possible. What He prays in John 17:20–23 is remarkable:

> I do not pray for these alone, but also for those who will believe in Me through their word; that they all may be one, as You, Father, are in Me, and I in You; that they also may be one in Us, that the world may believe that You sent Me. And the glory which You gave Me I have given them, that they may be one just as We are one: I in them, and You in Me; that they may be made perfect in one, and that the world may know that You have sent Me, and have loved them as You have loved Me.

This is where I derived the core theme of this book—not from a prophetic word or a covenantal promise, though either of these would be sufficient to build my faith. There is something different, however, about the recorded prayer of the God-Man, the Second Person of the Trinity made flesh, just before He goes to the cross to suffer and die for the sin of the world and the redemption of all mankind. This is the single most intimate moment of His life that we know of, and these words are the nearest to His heart, representing all that He wants from His Father in heaven.

Just prior to the cross, Jesus is praying for you and me to receive the same love—the same quality of love—that the Father enjoys with the Son, and the Son with the Father. Jesus is praying for you and me to have the same enjoyment, pleasure and joy in our relationship with one another as we do with God, and as God has within Himself. Jesus is praying that this expression of love would show the world that He was sent by His Father, was from the Father, and returned to the Father to prepare a place for us all to dwell together with Him. This is more than a prayer for Christian unity among a few churches in a city, working together to coordinate a few outreaches. This is a prayer for the highest and deepest expression of love possible between human beings in union with Christ by the indwelling of the Holy Spirit.

This fiery seal of divine love is God's grace for His presence on our hearts like a living flame, empowering us to love God and one another with all of our heart, soul, mind and strength *in actuality*. There will be available power, according to the recorded prayer of the Son of God, for our human hearts to love God with the entirety of our being, with all our conscious thoughts, and with every ounce of our strength, to our last breath. That kind of available grace and empowerment is coming to the Church. The end of the Shulamite's story—mature partnership, the seal of love, the spirit of prayer—all of it awaits us as the Bride in the future if the prayer of Jesus is something we take seriously. Jesus meant it when He prophesied, *"You shall love the Lord your God . . . !"*

The question for all of us in this hour is, What are we going to do about it? How are we going to respond? When I look at the social media arguments of today's bored and distracted Church, a Church hiding behind its pain and frustration with others in weakness, all of it an unpleasant distraction, I believe that none of it is moving us toward our day of triumph, none of it is imparting beauty or fascinating our hearts. When I hear Jesus pray, however, I am filled with a different kind of resolve about my future and what it can be. The question remains: What am I going to do about it?

I consider it my top priority to reform myself before I reform the Church around me. I see repentance as my main assignment and perseverance as my way forward as I wait on the Lord. Yet as I wait on Him to deliver me and escort me into new places of love and beauty, I want to prioritize having the knowledge of God and a fascinated heart. I don't want to be content with distraction and the petty, trivial matters that are part of a fading society. I want to make love for Jesus and for others my highest aim, and I want to invite the conviction of the Holy Spirit and the loving discipline of the Lord into my life whenever I wander off course a bit.

I will wander off course quite a bit, and quite often. I will be drawn away again, and then drawn back in, and there I will sign up to pursue Him again. I will do it knowing that He will "press delete" on my recent failures or distraction. He will not define me by how well I've pursued or not pursued Him recently. I do that; He does not. He sees the bigger picture. I must fight to do the same. I am content to know that perseverance in the smallness of today sets me on a collision course with a profound mystery. As I make my way, slowly, incrementally, in the simplicity of today's available grace to love and see His beauty, I will partner with that grace to orient my heart toward what will surely be a sudden, surprising breakthrough moment.

God is, and always will be, the God of *slowly, day-by-day,* and the God of *suddenly, all at once.* I engage by faith today, to be ready to run with passion and perseverance tomorrow. I am comforted by the many others, as weak as I am and as small and simple, who will be joining me on that day, in the fullness of the glory of His Church, the ultimate statement of His beauty and majesty on earth.

Amen.

NOTES

Chapter 5 From Brokenness to Beauty

1. D. Martyn Lloyd-Jones, *Romans: The Law: Its Functions and Limits, Exposition of Chapters 7:1–8:4*, 1ˢᵗ ed. (Grand Rapids: Zondervan, 1971), 61.

Chapter 6 "There, I Will Give You My Love"

1. James Durham, *Clavis Cantici; Or, an Exposition of the Song of Solomon*, with a preface by Gavin Parker (George King, 1840; Los Angeles: HardPress Publishing, 2018), Kindle edition, chapter 5.

2. George Burrowes, *The Song of Solomon* (New Zealand: Titus Books, 2014), Kindle edition, chapter 5.

Chapter 7 The Rejection of God's Beauty

1. D. Martyn Lloyd-Jones, *Romans 2:1–3:20 The Righteous Judgment of God*, 2 vols. (Edinburgh: Banner of Truth, 1985), chapter 3.

Chapter 8 The Vindication of the Name of the Lord

1. A. W. Tozer, *The Knowledge of the Holy* (New York: HarperOne, 1978), 1.

Chapter 9 The Fearless Church and the Consummation of Beauty

1. Angela Tilby, *The Seven Deadly Sins: Their Origin in the Spiritual Teaching of Evagrius the Hermit* (London: SPCK Publishing, 2013) Kindle edition, chapter 10.

2. Jean-Charles Nault, *The Noonday Devil: Acedia, the Unnamed Evil of Our Times* (San Francisco: Ignatius Press, 2013), 71.

David Sliker has been an executive leader, speaker and author at the International House of Prayer missions base in Kansas City, Missouri, for over twenty years. He is the president of International House of Prayer University and ministers around the world to equip saints in prayer and intimacy with God, the power of the Holy Spirit, passion for the Scriptures and the proclamation of Jesus and His return. Learn more at davidsliker.com.

More from David Sliker

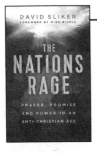

While the spiritual atmosphere grows more toxic and the world becomes more anti-God, Christians are engaging less with their faith in Christ and the power of the Holy Spirit. In this insightful book, David Sliker helps readers prepare for a future of glory, while unfolding the context of unprecedented rage, rebellion and resistance by the world around us.

The Nations Rage